J. Arthur Partridge

The making of the Irish nation

and the first-fruits of federation

J. Arthur Partridge

The making of the Irish nation
and the first-fruits of federation

ISBN/EAN: 9783744741026

Printed in Europe, USA, Canada, Australia, Japan

Cover: Foto ©ninafisch / pixelio.de

More available books at **www.hansebooks.com**

THE MAKING OF THE IRISH NATION:

AND

THE FIRST-FRUITS OF FEDERATION.

"Magnum rerum nascitur ordo"

BY

J. A. PARTRIDGE

Author of
"DEMOCRACY: ITS FACTORS AND CONDITIONS," "FROM FEUDAL TO FEDERAL," "THE POLICY OF ENGLAND IN RELATION TO INDIA AND THE EAST," ETC., ETC.

London
T FISHER UNWIN
26 PATERNOSTER SQUARE
—
1886

To the

TWO NATIONS

ENGLAND AND IRELAND

(THE ONE THE ELDER, THE OTHER THE MORE POWERFUL),

CONSTITUTING NOW IN GREAT BRITAIN AND IRELAND, IN CANADA, AUSTRALIA, AND THE COLONIES,

ONE EMPIRE;

AND TO THE ETERNAL MEMORIES OF MOLYNEUX, SWIFT, FLOOD, CURRAN, GRATTAN, BURKE, FOX, SHERIDAN, SHEIL, O'CONNELL, AND MANY OTHERS, THE MAKERS AND MARTYRS OF IRELAND, THIS VOLUME IS CONSECRATED.

PREFACE.

"Sometimes, it is true, a rare individual has appeared among us, raising a degraded country from the condition of a province to the rank and consequence of a people worthy to be the ally of a mighty empire, forming the league that bound her to Great Britain, on the firm and honourable basis of equal liberty and a common fate, standing and falling with the British Empire."—CURRAN.

"One word upon the legislative independence of Ireland—that which is now called a 'Repeal of the Union.' It is said to be a severance of the empire, a separation of the two countries. Illustrious lady, these statements are made by men who know them to be unfounded; an Irish legislative independence would, on the contrary, be the strongest and most durable connection between your Majesty's Irish and your British dominions. It would, by conciliating your Irish subjects, and attending to their wants and wishes, render the separation of Ireland from the lawful dominion of your Crown utterly impossible."—O'CONNELL's *Memoir Addressed to the Queen.*

"I think I can trace all the calamities of this country to the single source of our not having had steadily before our eyes a general, comprehensive, well-connected, and well-proportioned view of the whole of our dominions, and a just sense of their true bearings and relations. If we make ourselves too little for the sphere of our duty; if, on the contrary, we do not stretch and expand our minds to the compass of their object, be well assured that everything about us will dwindle by degrees, until at length our concerns are shrunk to the dimensions of our minds. The Parliament of Great Britain sits at the head of her extensive empire in two capacities—one, as the local legislature of this island, providing, &c.; the other, and I think her nobler capacity, in what I call her imperial character, in which, as from the throne of heaven, she superintends all the several inferior legislatures, and guides and controls them all, without annihilating any."—BURKE.

PREFACE.

"Without examining details, the whole of liberal Europe and America is loud in admiration of the initiative taken by the illustrious statesman."—EMILE DE LAVELEYE.

"She follows her physical destination, and obeys the dispensations of providence when she protests like that sea, against the two situations, both equally unnatural—separation and union. She feels her Constitution to be her great stake in the empire, and the empire the great security of her Constitution. If British ministers take away the Constitution, they withdraw at once a great pillar of liberty and empire."—GRATTAN.

"Should England not change her conduct, Ireland may still for a long period belong to her; but not always; and the loss of that country is the death-day, not only of her greatness, but her very existence."—NIEBUHR.

"High politics are like the pyramids, only two sorts of animals reach the top—reptiles and eagles."—D'ALEMBERT.

WE are in a transition state. Yesterday, we were an oligarchic republic (tempered by queen, chaos, and revolution); to-day, we are a democratic republic (a pyramid, resting for the most part on its base); to-morrow, we shall be members of an imperial democratic confederated empire, the most stupendous manifestation of order, economy, and power, yet possible on this planet; and whilst all things are getting forged and fitted to their places, men come up to see and wonder at this great sight, a mighty people, a royal nation, an imperial confederacy, depending not on its creatures, but on itself, nor intending ever again, for all or any of them, to run again the dread inane cycle of blood, ruin, and reaction.

It is all coming, because come it must. The fact is, we are at the fag end of a slave fight. We have let our overseers, Pitt, Peel, and Co., carry on, since 1782, the "hell harrowing" of Ireland, because in 1782 she happened to have, not a captain, but only orators and a parliament; and because we can't understand till it is licked into us, that any one but ourselves—and Polands and Italys a long way off—have rights. We want Home Rule in England. We can't make England, or Ireland, or the empire, without making Ireland, and if we don't begin soon it may be too late. Manhood rules here now, and rules for manhood and empire, not for property, slave-drivers, or things; and besides all that, the Puritans are waking up, and they are the real blood royal of England.

On the whole, our situation to-day is not unlike that of America, when making up its mind to put down the slave trade and to unite the empire—sketched so well by Wendell Phillips:

"I divide you into four sections. The first is the ordinary mass, rushing from mere enthusiasm to battle. Behind that class stands another, whose only idea in this controversy is Sovereignty and the flag. Next to it stands the third element, the people—the broad surface of the people, who have no time for technicalities, who never studied law, who never had time to read further into the Constitution than the first two lines, 'Establish justice and secure liberty.' They have waited long enough; they have eaten dirt enough; they have apologized for bankrupt statesmen enough; they have quieted their consciences enough; and now they have got their hand on the neck of a rebellious aristocracy, and in the name of the people mean to strangle it.

"That I believe is the body of the people itself. Side by side with them stands a fourth class—small, but active—the abolitionists, who thank God that He has let them see His salvation before they die."

With us, the slaves and the slave-drivers are not in the same country. With us, the "rebellious aristocracy," and "the bankrupt statesmen," have hardly yet gone under; but "the people have waited long enough, eaten dirt enough, apologized enough, and quieted their consciences enough" for them. All the people are going to do now, however, is to wrench these bankrupt statesmen from the throats of the Irish nation.

It is our duty now to make to Ireland certain concessions, but duty soon will be something else in the world-logic of nation and empire. A little more tomfoolery about Ireland, and events themselves will pronounce the philosophers played out, and demand "room for the men of destiny."

The ultimate facts between us and Ireland are that Ireland must soon hold ten millions of souls, that the ten millions of other Irish elsewhere will soon become twenty millions—subscribing, aspiring, and, if they must, avenging—with cosmopolitan sympathies, with American drill and arms, and Irishmen in England enough to command sixty or seventy boroughs, to say nothing of foreign war.

Besides all this, England is in a more factitious state than Ireland, which has to fill up and grow in greater ratio than England can. Not one-fourteenth of Ireland is uncultivatable, and she is nearer the west, and with mightier harbours. From Connaught to the Kentish coast is none too wide a base for the world-weighted glories of the empire of Cromwell and Shakespeare, of Wyclif and Milton, of Raleigh, Wesley, Chatham, Cobden, and Burke.

I recur here to what I wrote "On Democracy" in 1864, and in "From Feudal to Federal" in 1872:

"A false conservatism dreads each advance as approaching the final anarchy, but if the progressive universal power in politics be a delusion, then, not development, but restraint is the true gospel, and there is a hitch somewhere, not only in democracy, but in creation. Every government tends to some preponderating power or to anarchy, and the organization of democracy is of necessity the problem of every advancing age and people. Thus a true nation itself becomes a unit, and is alone fit to enter with other nations into those grander combinations for which the world prepares. Organizations are really a hierarchy, and must rise from 'the local unit of the commune and parish, to county, province, nation, and empire. In all governments there is the virtual proponderating power that is the power which would prevail if things were forced to an issue, and the actual Constitution is or is not in danger, as it is or is not in harmony with the real power."

In this view of the federal question, Professor Dicey and others have lately talked in a rather helpless way about our imperial Constitution as binding Australia or Canada; as though a Constitution, which, in case of strain could not constitute, could settle the principle of any such problem. The question is hardly a political one, even for academicians, "How to arrange so that the preponderating power shall not preponderate"!

The intenser nationality question being in principle settled, the broader and supreme remaining question is the constitutional one—What is to be the link between nation and empire? In other words, the supreme question is the federal one; and the difficulty is that the Irish question has precipitated the federal, almost before the masses have had time to realize that it is the federal. The one thing certain is that we may take advantage of the situation to make Ireland the first-fruits of federation. Ireland, Canada, Australia, and, let us hope, a South African confederation, have to be brought into working constitutional relations with each other through and with Great Britain. The present chaos between the Lords and the people, between the empires and nations that are to be federated with one another and Great Britain, and the confusion in weak men's minds between local self-government and national self-government—all this has to be altered. The Lords must be made a real Second Chamber, if there is to be one, or if empire is to be represented in it; and, in any event, some mixed ratio of population, wealth, and contribution to the general defence, has to be fixed on as the basis of imperial representation; whilst local self-government in Scotland and Wales, the counties, and London, must ease the central machine.

Of all this change, vast in detail, simple though momentous in principle, the settlement of the Irish federal question ought to be the first-fruits and defence.

In America and Canada there were no nations to come together and agree—there were States and provinces, and vast unpeopled wilds.

In Canada, Australia, Ireland, we have nations already made, and it is childish to suppose they can be treated as other than what they are.

The fact is, circumstances such as those we have to consider have never been dealt with, or even existed, before — the distances, the vast territories, the coming enormous population. There are, however, odds in favour of an imperial, and almost a cosmopolitan, unity that never existed before—English traditions and the spirit of English citizenship, unity of race to a great extent, unity of language, unity or similarity of institution, a common history, and the fact that the public thought, life, and opinion of England is to so great an extent the thought, life, and opinion of the civilized world.

Representatives in London, Ireland must of course have, if only to prepare for federation. There should be 32, because that would constitute at once about the quota due from Ireland when Canada, Australia, &c., are represented in an Imperial Federal Parliament, and because 32 would give one representative for each county. The 32 might be elected either by the Dublin Parliament or by the counties.

But we must cut our federal coat according to the confederal cloth, and not pretend that because States may coalesce better than nations, therefore we ought to treat nations as States.

The principles of all these questions were discussed,

sifted, and acted on by the great men who made the American nation, in a way and with a clearness, sincerity, and depth that make them the best authorities in the world on federal and kindred subjects, whilst Pitt shows beside them as a satyr to Hyperion.

Said Hamilton, in *The Federalist:*

"However gross a heresy it may be that a party to a compact has a right to revoke that compact, the possibility shows the necessity of laying the foundation of our national government deeper than in the mere sanction of delegated authority. The fabric of American authority ought to rest on the solid basis of the consent of the people."

Said Patrick Henry, at the Virginian Convention, 1788:

"Have they said, 'We, the States'? Have they made a proposal of compact between States? If they had, this would be a confederation; it is otherwise, most clearly, a consolidated government."

Said Chancellor Kent:

"The plan was submitted to a convention of delegates, chosen by the people at large in each State for assent and ratification. Such a measure was laying the foundation of the fabric of our national polity where alone they ought to be laid, on the broad consent of the people."

Said Chief Justice Storey:

"A fundamental law, a supreme rule, which no State was at liberty to disregard, to suspend, or to annul."

Henry Clay said: "I owe a paramount allegiance to the whole union, a subordinate one to my own State;" and Madison repeatedly and emphatically declared that "the resolutions were intended to claim, not for an individual State, but for the United States, the right of remedying its abuses in constitutional ways."

When States make an empire, *that* is an orthodox, old-fashioned federation; when the people make it, *there* is a consolidated government. But no precedent will exactly fit the Anglo-Irish problem.

Lord Brougham, on the United States Government, put this clearly as to States:

"The proper federal union is where two or more States, having their separate governments for all domestic purposes, are united by a central government, which regulates their mutual relations as members of a political community, but does not interfere with the functions of the several governments and their authority over the individuals which are their subjects, unless in so far as those functions and that authority may affect the federal relation. There must be certain things which cannot be altered without universal consent."

And Madison, April 8, 1787, put the converse axiom:

"I hold it a fundamental point that the individual independence of the States is utterly irreconcilable with the idea of an aggregate sovereignty. Let the national government have a negative. Without such a defensive power, every positive power that can be given on paper will be unavailing."

For "national" in Madison, read "imperial" for ourselves; and that emphasizes the fact that it will never do to consider *a priori* what makes strong or weak governments, and then say we will have such and such an arrangement, without seeing that we have the corresponding materials. If we do, we shall get upset. For in Ireland we have to do with a nation already made, whereas in America, "the States," as Madison asserted, "never possessed the essential rights of sovereignty, having the power of making by-laws, effectual only, if not contradictory, to the general confederation."

Of course we have to avoid the establishment of that "constituted anarchy" of which Hegel complained in Germany, "a totality, with private rights to contradict the whole."

All this is clear; and as Chancellor Kent explained in his Commentaries, "the incurable defects of all former federal governments were that they were sovereignties over sovereignties;" that is to say, translated for our own situation—That one nation, the English, should dominate another, the Irish, were an "incurable defect," no doubt. But then, I repeat, it is not, cannot be, that the English nation will attempt anything of the sort. It is the imperial delegation that will, as De Tocqueville explained of America, dominate the sections:

"The Constitution rests upon a novel theory, which may be considered a great invention of political science. In all confederations formed before 1789, the allied States reserved to themselves the right of ordaining and enforcing the laws of the union. The American States agreed that the Federal Government should not only dictate the laws, but execute its own enactments. This alteration produced the most momentous consequences."

All the American State constitutions recognize three things—certain inalienable rights of the people; the right to change according to pre-established rules by the vote of a certain majority; and the duty to obey until that change is effected.

If we deny the first, we strike against the rock of ultimate power and appeal. We shall have to settle the mode of change, and to acknowledge the duty to obey.

The mode and conditions of change were regulated for America by Article 13 of the Confederation, and by Article 5 of the United States Constitution:

"Nor shall any alteration at any time hereafter be made in any of them, unless such alteration be agreed to in a Congress of the United States; and be afterwards confirmed by the legislatures of every State."[1]

"The Congress, whenever two-thirds of both Houses shall deem it necessary, shall propose amendments to this Constitution,

---

[1] Article 13 of Confederation.

or, on the application of the legislatures of two-thirds of the several States, shall call a Convention for proposing amendments, &c."[1]

Madison stated the general principle that organization is a hierarchy, and that all laws contrary to the spirit of the whole must be made and treated only as by-laws:

"There is a gradation of power in all societies, from the lowest corporation to the highest sovereign. The States have the power of making by-laws effectual only if not contradictory to the general confederation."

So that the whole question is, Do we want to make a whole or not, and what whole? Are we to confederate, or to remain defenceless and disorganized in the face of other coming colossal combinations?

As I said, the federal question is the supreme one, and it cannot be shelved or shirked.

Montesquieu long ago explained how, in every combination, there is "a spirit of the whole" which must be conformed to. Are we then to subside, or to seek "the goal of this irresistible urging"?

Let Washington wind up this constitutional question:

"To the efficacy and permanency of your union a government for the whole is indispensable. No alliance, however strict, between the parts, can be an adequate substitute; they must inevitably experience the infractions and interruptions which all alliances, in all time, have experienced.

"The basis of your political systems is the right of the people to make and to alter their constitutions of government; but the constitution which at any time exists, till changed by an explicit and authentic act of the whole people, is sacredly obligatory upon all. The very idea of the power and right of the people to establish government, presupposes the duty of every individual to obey the established government."[2]

[1] Article 5 United States Constitution.
[2] Washington's Farewell.

Now Mr. Gladstone has not appealed to "States" that are to make a nation, but to nations that are to make an empire, and the future federation will be strong, because living nations make it; whilst divisions will be avoided or settled by representatives of the great federal communities, informed and inspired by the almost universal spirit of British citizenship.

American federalists made the future nation by fair, free, and philosophic arrangements, which breathed an exalted and invincible citizenship into the hearts of the millions who were to come to her from every tyranny and every clime. We must take Ireland as she is—about a third the size of Great Britain, with the most intense nationality, a large territory, a sea and ocean frontier—too near to be separate, too far from us to be mechanically united. If we do not want to be wiser than nature and God, we shall get along well enough. Federation may or may not make a weak Government, it all depends. Partisans and sciolists are always the victims of words. Gladstone makes a statutory parliament—granted; but who makes Gladstone make it? Who and what inspires him? The Irish nation, and the spirit of the future, to which he so exquisitely refers. We have tried to destroy that nation, physically, materially, commercially, politically, and spiritually for centuries, and we have found it indestructible. The nation is there, twenty million acres are there, there are her mountains, rivers, harbours, soil, and sea. There is the disposition to be grateful, there is the policy, inherited from Grattan and from Burke, to unite; here is the opportunity also, and God forgive those who palter with the issues! It is not "we, the States," who meet together and theorize, and who might form a flimsy superstructure—or weak Government—it is "we," the two nations and the Empire. It is a policy of progress and hope, instinct with all the forces and passions God can put into a nation, and based upon ample geographical, political, and material guarantees of real union. "We, the people" of England, make the Irish Parliament, and will make such a parliament as befits the great and glorious nationality that God and the Irish have already made. If we sow thus, we shall reap centralization thorough enough as to foreign policy, and decentralization enough also. The Irish Establishment gone, "the Castle" disendowed, nationality appeased, why should not the whole sacred force and passion of the men of Ireland, England, and the Empire have free course and be glorified?

It may be natural for Orange ascendency to dislike Catholic equality, especially with those whom Orangemen have always treated as inferior in race, nationality, and religion; but the double principles of nationality and equality cannot fail, as they did even in the slave States of America, to win their way. Nationality and equality are the intensest political passions, and once they are given free sway, Protestantism is certainly not a likely principle to help Ulster in repeating the part of the "mean whites" of the South in their slave crisis.

Neither Orangemen who are not Irishmen, nor Irishmen who are not Ulstermen, need fear English partizanship or unfairness, for this simple reason—Irish affairs, when not settled in Ireland, will come to be dominated not by England, but by the Empire. It is the federal power that will interfere when there must be interference; it is the federal power that will mould also imperial federal politics. The sovereignty in imperial matters will pass away from England and Ireland both, to become vested in the delegates of empire. Ireland, of course, must settle her own "by-laws."

There is, I hope, in these pages, everything really necessary to a fair understanding of the essential Irish question, past and present, and of its dawning national and federal future; there is also, I trust, nothing superfluous or overlaboured to prevent its becoming a handbook for the people.

Five years ago, seeing the crisis coming, and having always advocated recognition of the principle of Irish nationality, I made a fresh study of the Irish speeches of Grattan, Burke, and Fox. Of course, with these great men, the making of the nation and empire were one cause, process, and question. We find, however, dismemberment, disruption, and separation charged upon them and ourselves.

I then read the definite compact and treaty of peace between the two nations conducted by Grattan and Fox, assented to by the four Houses, the Premier and Viceroy, and to which George III. personally pledged himself; but this we are now told had no validity. Next came the enlightened, fair-dealing legislation of Grattan's Parliament, as good as Castlereagh's corruption and Pitt's brutality would let it be, and the evidence of the prosperity which follows freedom. I then traced the stimulated divisions between Catholic and Protestant; the disintegration of the volunteer force; and finally, to carry the Union, the exchange of Irish troops for English, and the making public meetings felony. But we are told that Grattan's Parliament was a failure, the Union a success, and that the large exports, since 1800, of food the Irish wanted prove the prosperity of Ireland, and the success of the Union! Next there came the frightful consequences of Pitt's handiwork—his massacres, tortures, evictions, famines; I reflected on the yearning and striving, ever since Molyneux and Swift, for nationality, their misery for seven hundred years; but the answer came, "It is not every nation that is fit for self-government," and "the Irish have no political genius or fixed resolve."

Was there, then, any possible mistake? How is it that Ireland has not asserted herself? An English Premier has given the only answer: "The only remedy was revolution, and the Irish could not make one." The toad under the harrow had a better chance than Ireland under Whig or Tory. Grattan's Parliament succeeded too much. Catholics were not represented that the Irish Church Establishment might be maintained. The garrison church, province, and junto helped to maintain each other, and Ireland became an English barracks.

O'Connell said, in 1843, all that was necessary to prove that Ireland was a nation, and that she cannot, ought not, and dare not fail to assert her nationality, and I summarize his speech in "The Argument." As to the sectional and superfine gentlemen who learn and remember nothing, it is not necessary to answer them. It is past their province to settle anything. They are superseded. They never were anything, and never represented anything, and will soon be nothing. Two years ago Mr. Gladstone appealed to a new political world to redress the balances of the old, and two months ago he appealed bodily for a mandate to the English nation. The moment politics came into touch with the aggregate manhood, they came into touch with reality, with the people, with the two nations, with the empire, and also with the federal instinct and principle. The work of Molyneux, Swift, and Grattan was taken up where they left it, and the English and Irish nations shook hands across the gulf of centuries. Nation always sympathizes with nation, when their common factor manhood can really rule. Politics based on property and things are used for property and things, and that is what we have been doing in Ireland—farming out law, land, religion, and nation on behalf of property, and pretences, and against the national manhood and life. Such politics are radically and eternally illegitimate, for property ruling manhood is the servant ruling his master. The hour has come and the man, whose imperial Radicalism has already turned the old political world upside down—setting the new one on its base instead of on its apex, and who will soon turn the old political lumber-room of "the Castle"—and other places—inside out. His appeal now is to the disciplined reason of the educated few, and to the undebauched instincts of the whole English people—to those by whom the great principles of nationality and empire are always believed in and always understood.

Three persistent fallacies confound and perplex the issues of the Anglo-Irish question. The first is that, in the case of Ireland, prosperity followed slavery, and a vast increase of imports and exports, the union. The second is that the province of Ulster, having a majority of Protestants, may become the victim of Roman Catholic tyranny, and has a right to demand separate legislation and autonomy, and to prevent the integration of the nation. The third is that to qualify, to beset with conditions, or to grudgingly admit the nationality of Ireland, is to make her a better or safer helpmate, or a sounder member of our coming confederation; and we have accordingly rather mixed analogies from the federations of the world, misfitted and misapplied to the very special case of England and Ireland.

The first fallacy is a very old and a very foolish one. As O'Connell argued, *is it likely* that the sort of relations forced upon Ireland, and the sort of statesmanship applied to her by Pitt and Peel, should promote prosperity? The figures are admitted—were admitted as soon as they could well be got together—by "Mr. Wm. Irving, Inspector-General of Imports and Exports, dating from his office at the Custom-house, January 15, 1831." The tables all appear in the appendices to Sir Henry Parnell's book on "Financial Reform," and I refer to them in the sequel. The answer to the prosperity theory, founded on increased exports, is, that unless Irishmen are entirely different from other people, it does them no good to have the things they most want sent out of their country. No doubt imports and exports increased from 1790 to 1826 and 1830, and no doubt somebody benefited by them; but that is not national prosperity, and if it were, what is the wonder that in those forty years, with or without the Union, imports and exports increased?

The allegation, on such grounds, of national prosperity, is hardly worth notice. The fact is, the Irish had to send out of the country the things they most wanted, and the better the things were and the more they wanted them the more they couldn't get them. And that is "prosperity"! and it resulted from the Union! The tables of articles "retained" in Ireland tell a very different story from that of articles sent out of Ireland, which ought to have been kept in. Taking round numbers, and triennial periods from 1790 to 1826 or 1830, the consumption of tea a little more than doubled, that of coffee was multiplied thirteen times, and that of sugar and coals doubled. But then the consumption of coffee began with only 44,370lbs. for five or six millions of population.

The export of oxen, bacon and hams, swine, and sheep, multiplied three, twenty, thirteen, and more than sixty-fold respectively, and that of wheat more than twelve-fold. The only thing to be said is, that this is the sort of prosperity Tory government generally secures—it takes the good things away from the people.

With regard to Ulster, I can only here summarize what is shown further on. Pitt deliberately reopened and fostered feelings of hostility and division. Ulstermen were petted and rewarded as partners in, and abettors of, tyranny and proscription. In 1793, sectarian hatred had been cast out, and had died down, till the whole nation demanded that Catholics sit in parliament. Pitt saw what would follow that, and never swerved afterwards in his efforts at destroying and dividing the Irish people. At least since Grattan, and specially under O'Connell's teaching, Catholics have been conciliatory and Orangemen dictatorial. I do not, of course, speak of men dying of hunger, or mad with despair.

With Nationalists a majority in Parliament, with a strong minority of Catholics, with the Home Rule Association just formed in Belfast, and considering Mr. Gladstone's safeguard for minorities, our entire control of army and navy, and that some Irish representatives will no doubt continue to sit at Westminster, there will be nothing for Ulster to fight for.

The third fallacy is that there is, or can be, anything naturally uncanny, or dangerous, or disloyal in the temper of a nation like the Irish towards conciliatory fellow-citizens, or towards a protecting and friendly neighbour like England. Development, not repression, is the liberal gospel, and development on the right natural lines is the only true conservatism.

It dilates our conceptions, dim though they may be, vast as they must be, of the mighty unknown future of the coming democratic confederation of all the Britains, into which Ireland, equal among equals, now enters, to believe, as we must, that Ireland's past sufferings are not to be compared with the exceeding weight of glory of her national and of our common federal future—the next step but one, probably, in the world-logic of events, to the founding of the universal commonwealth. As God is faithful, as nations are sacred, as humanity is one, we must believe this for Ireland, and we may believe it for ourselves, if, as Gladstone now says, we are faithful to our imperial and not to our Irish traditions. For if man is made of one blood by a Being who foresaw and knew all, a democracy and a civilization wide as the world, and part of something even more lasting and universal, is preparing for us.

The Tories are the Calvinists of politics. Themselves the elect of the Fortunate Isles, they view with composure the millions of the socially and politically predestined "damned, 'whelmed in the whirling flood;" and they say, as Macaulay said, as false political economists have said, as Pitt and Peel, and everybody except the thinkers and the people, except Gladstone and the new English nation, and the martyrs and makers of Ireland have said, "The misery of Ireland is necessary to the mastery of Britain" —the political slavery of the many to the political salvation of the few.

Whigs and Tories fog everything and fetter everything, because they do not know and cannot conceive that a true, real, complete nation is, and must be, a better and truer ally than an incomplete and faulty one. There is no future for their politics, because there is no truth, largeness, or depth in their conceptions either of manhood, the only political force, or of nationhood, the only political royalty.

Whigs want a constitutional balance, and cannot conceive that there is always a preponderating power which will not balance; Tories want absolute power, and cannot see that the only power in politics is manhood, its only conservatism a complete and an equable development.

This is the difference between the men of the dawn and of the night—a greater difference than that between the "reptiles and the eagles," which both alike in politics reach the summit.

The political past of Tories and Whigs makes for us all the difficulties we now inherit. To get rid of their bias in the opening future would make all the difference between the political heavens and earth. Their career is, however, for Ireland nearly over. The future of politics will soon see their breed extinct, and in the name of

England and Ireland, both, we address to them words, in this instance as true as they are classic: "Ye have eaten enough, ye have drunken enough, ye have wantoned enough; it is time for ye to depart!"

J. A. PARTRIDGE.

Oxford, and Reform Club, S.W.
July, 1886.

CONTENTS.

	PAGE
THE ARGUMENT	3
IRELAND A NATION	29
IRELAND BETRAYED	59
NATIONAL RESURRECTION	101

THE MAKING OF THE IRISH NATION.

"The ocean protests against separation, and the sea against union."—GRATTAN.

"The great trident that was to move the world must be grasped by England alone. Independence of legislature had been granted to Ireland, but no other independence could Great Britain give her without reversing the order of nature. Ireland could not be separated from England; she could not exist without her; she must ever remain under the protection of England, her guardian angel."—BURKE, in debate, May 19, 1785, on Pitt's resolutions relating to commercial arrangements with Ireland.

"When a people have the boundaries and history, the separate characters and physical resources, and, still more, the virtue and genius of a nation, they are bound in conscience, in prudence, and in wisdom to assert their individuality, no matter how conciliation may lure or armies threaten."—*The Teaching of* "*The Nation,*" 1843.

"I laid down five and five only essential conditions. The first was unity of empire; the second was political equality; the third was equitable distribution of imperial burdens; the fourth was protection of minorities; the fifth was that the measure should present the essential character of a settlement."—The RIGHT HON. W. E. GLADSTONE, May 10, 1886 (*Times* report).

"When it was determined to confer home rule on Canada, Canada was in the precise temper attributed to Ireland. She did not get home rule because she was loyal and friendly, but she is loyal and friendly because she has got home rule."—SIR CHARLES GAVAN DUFFY.

"Every civilized country is entitled to settle its internal affairs in its own way, and no other country ought to interfere with its discretion, because one country, even with the best intentions, has no chance of properly understanding the internal affairs of another."—J. S. MILL, *Letter on the Westminster Election*, 1868.

"A nationality which shall inflame and purify our people with a lofty and heroic love of country—a nationality of the spirit as well as of the letter—a nationality which may come to be stamped upon our manners, our literature, and our deeds—which may embrace Protestant, Catholic, and Dissenter, Milesian and Cromwellian—the Irishman of a hundred generations and the stranger who is within our gates."—*Prospectus of "The Nation,"* 1843.

"The real root is the want of national institutions, of a national capital and life. Everything patriotic is rebellious."—GOLDWIN SMITH.

"Union is not unity. Heterogeneous and repugnant things may be arbitrarily tied together, but this is not unity. 'Union' has no assimilating power. Closer contact elicits the repugnances which rend all external bonds asunder."—CARDINAL MANNING.

"In the case of Ireland, as truly as in that of Poland, a national constitution was destroyed by a foreign power, contrary to the wishes of the people. It was a crime of treachery and corruption. Few things are more discreditable to political English literature than the tone of palliation. Scarcely any element or aggravation of political immorality was wanting, and the term honour, if applied to Pitt and Castlereagh, ceases to have any real meaning in politics. The union, as carried, was crime of the deepest turpitude; every circumstance of infamy vitiated the whole course of Irish opinion. Generation after generation, by a slow, steady, fatal process, the nation has been educated into disloyalty, taught to distrust constitutional means, and to regard outrage as invariable prelude to concession."—LECKY on *Grattan*, pp. 182, 183.

"Ireland was, in fact, a foreign country; we preferred to assume that she was an integral part of the empire. . . . At the conquest we forced the Irish Church into submission to the papacy. At the Reformation we forced it to apostatize. . . . The theory of our Church Establishment split the garrison of Protestants into hostile camps. A free representative legislature which . . . was not free and was not representative; a gentry who could not rule; a Church which could not teach; laws which could not be enforced. . . . If the object was to absorb and extinguish the spirit of Irish nationality, it singularly failed. . . . Had the union been conceded for which the presentiments of the Irish Parliament led them to petition in 1704; had trade and manufactures been allowed to develop, and the stream of British Protestant emigration been directed continuously into all parts of the island, the native population might have been overborne or driven out, and the mother country might have retained the affections of a people with whom she would then have been identified in interest and sentiment."—FROUDE'S *English in Ireland*, book v. pp. 2, 3.

THE MAKING OF THE IRISH NATION.

CHAPTER I.

THE ARGUMENT.

"Tell your countrymen that your connection with England is the source of her liberty and a means of her greatness; make them proud of standing by England. Tell them that all their passions and interests can be completely gratified, and that the boldest exercise of freedom is perfectly conformable to the closest bonds of the British connection. Nations are governed, not by interest only, but by passion, and the passion of Ireland is freedom. So much her passion is, that a wise monarch who loved power would reject the proffer of her servitude, and set her free to command her absolutely."—GRATTAN.

"We should start upon two principles: first, respect for nationalities—a principle of justice; and secondly, the maintenance of the power and greatness of England—a condition essential to the general progress of our Western world. Beyond a federal *régime*, based on a solid foundation. . . . I see nothing in the horizon but a war of secession."—M. EMILE DE LAVELEYE.

"In fact, the union was not only a great crime, but a great blunder."—LECKY.

"Pitt's connection with the great Tory party made it easy for him to proscribe the Roman Catholics, to torture the suspected, to burn the houses of the peasantry. But when he sought to admit the Roman Catholics to parliament and office, &c., the same Tory party, headed by the king, put an insuperable bar in the way of his endeavours."—EARL RUSSELL'S *Life and Times of Fox*, book iii. p. 141.

THE making of a nation is a greater event than any other can be, save the making of a world. It is the mightiest, most glorious, and most august achievement, and the longest and most difficult process possible on this planet; only less august than the making of the planet itself. When such a fact is really accomplished the world should rejoice at it, and all nations hasten to acknowledge it.

For it is the supremacy of centripetal, conservative, creative, constructive, social and political forces, over centrifugal destructive ones, throughout one of the largest areas, and in one of the most important individualities of the world's great vicinage. Working downwards and inwards, a nation is built up of its counties, municipalities, communes, the whole being based upon the free individual manhood of the country: working outwards, a true nation alone can take its place in those vaster conglomerates of economy, freedom, peace, and power, which the future must establish, and of which the English Empire is the most conspicuous instance.

In becoming a willing portion of such an empire, each constituent nation must of course yield something; but it need never—must never—yield that sort of representation which is the vital link and living bond of the whole.

In falling within the orbit of a star of greater magnitude, it must of course revolve around it, but it still revolves on its own axis; it is more complete within, and more powerful without; there is cosmos instead of chaos, and sublimer order instead of the crash of colliding worlds.

All organization is a hierarchy, and as nations can only become self-governing and royal when based upon manhood, the only political force; so empires can only securely stand when the nations of which they are made are really royal.

To make the Britannic Empire, we English mean to make the Irish nation; and in making the Irish nation, the Irish will help to make the empire. The two processes are one, and Gladstone rightly heralded them by basing both on their represented manhood; but the safety of the rule or order of future life between the two nations, depends first upon seeing clearly that they are two nations who have to settle that rule and order. Words must not be mistaken for things, or forms for force, and practical men must clear their minds at least of so much cant as is already found out, or likely to be found out, respecting the practical dominant forces of the situation.

A Constitution is strong and lasting according to the real strength and truth upon which it is based, and statesmanship considers and sees what is that strength now, what it is certain to be soon, and what it must be later. The constitutional Convention is the American proviso for change; ours is a General Election. But we must not forget that force is always the last remedy, nor that when the Senate (two senators for each State) of the great democracy proved too conservative for free men to live with, and when the Chief Justice (Dred Scott and other decisions) became the arch thief of the Republic, the final problem had to be solved—are honest men stronger than thieves, and is truth grounded on the people? *Le droit prime la force;* but if not, nation and right go down together, and the appeal lies to the whole and to the future. The problem of false statesmen, like Pitt, is how to found immorality upon weakness; and his solution of it, as it shook hell with laughter, has shaken England and Ireland with revolution ever since.

After eighty-six years the judgment has come, the books once more are open, and the appeal this time is to the people of both nations. It comes, for us Englishmen, from Pitt and George III., and the three oligarchies of Whig landlord junto, and garrison Church and province, to the nation, to Victoria, and to Gladstone, who has the mandate of both; and as the wrong will not now be sustained by the English nation, the Irish nation will get its own, as will also the English Empire and people. The problem solving in politics always is how right shall be preserved, or how the policy and the politician shall be destroyed; the destruction is a provincial question, each country can settle it for itself; the right is an imperial question, providence secures it for the whole.

"To build upon a rock," said Napoleon, "means to establish government on the democratic principle." "Let no one quote the old maxim against me," said Machiavel, "that 'whosoever builds upon the people builds upon the sand.'" "The people at large," said Aristotle, "may always quash the vain pretences of the few, by saying, 'We collectively are richer, wiser, and nobler than you.'" And the French poet is no less faithful and strong; for "each combination of ashes returns to ashes; all those granites, oligarchy, aristocracy, (if not) theology, are promised to the four winds." We build our future not on the sectional, the superfine, or the superficial; but, on the eternal granite of the universal people, and on the sense of justice and right, the charity, pathos, sympathy, and love, begotten in their hearts by the daily expenditure of work and effort—that is, of themselves, in keeping, and in helping one another to keep, hearthstone and roof, soul and body together.

Useless to talk to them of Ireland as anything but what she is and where she is—to draw conclusions of what might be, were Ireland linked to the Continent, or far from England, or near to America; or as if she were one of many united or untied States, or of a new Dominion. Ireland is a country of over 20,000,000 acres (a fourth size of England); has fed 8,000,000 souls, and might soon feed as many as England did when she contended against embattled Europe; she has a distinct frontier, a fertile soil, great rivers, splendid harbours, a noble race, and a popular religion; she is moored alongside England is shielded—she ought to be—by England's mighty headland from mightier dangers elsewhere. She is due west of England sixty-seven miles, and three or four hours from Holyhead; she is not Belgium or Hanover, or in America or Canada, and she has had the principle of a settlement offered her, a settlement safely and finally based on what she is—a nation —by their man of destiny and of the epoch—Gladstone.

It will be the work now of the two nations to let the future of Ireland translate into politics the hieroglyphics of God, foreshadowed in the facts of nature, and written on the face of history. It may be the attempt of traitors and fools to establish a policy of suicide for England, whilst proffering to our sister nation a policy of revolution and despair. For we also in England have our counterfeit presentments of Senates conservative of wrong, and a party both for and against Home Rule; we have our House of Lords, we have our shrieking marquis, and another marquis, of right English fibre and intent, but descended from one of those three families that for a century made good government in Ireland impossible. Still, thank God, we have not now, as in 1800, an oligarchy in absolute possession of the resources of the three kingdoms, and offering, as did the clear-seeing South, "to rend God's moral government from turret to foundation," though doing it not as the South, but in God's own name, and in that of His Church and king.

The Irish question involves three cardinal questions. The first is Irish nationality—the right of a nation to govern itself from its own capitol, which no Liberal will deny. The second is unity of empire. As nations are made up of free, self-governing sections, and finally of free men, so empires are made up of free nations. The third question is that of the link between nation and empire. Constituent nations can alone join with one another in making their empire, and can alone make their empire in joining with one another. What is to be the link? What the outward and visible constitutional form? If there be none for Ireland, then the question is insoluble. For her to assume the present status of Colonial independence is absolutely impossible. She is too near for an independence that is not federal, and she is once for all and for ever a nation.

The federal question is not ripe, but it is getting ready to ripen, and meanwhile nothing should be done to prejudice and everything to facilitate federation. Ireland can only join the empire, and the other nations that make the empire, by sending to the imperial senate her quota of imperial representatives. What will be that senate and how many those representatives has yet to appear; but the principle is certain and definite. The representatives of empire should not be the same men, nor should they be elected in the same way, as the representatives of Irish or other boroughs. They should be elected by the national representatives; they should be in numbers something like Ireland's future quota to the Imperial Federal Council-chamber, for which the present "upper" chamber will have to be swept and garnished. This, or something like it, cannot fail to come as between our imperial independencies and England, and it is because it has not come, and yet is coming, that we differ in detail; it is because it has got to come throughout, and because Ireland may and should now be made the first-fruits of federation, that the principle of the federal link should be foreshadowed and affirmed.

The controversy between the English and Irish nations has been interminable, because we have declined to accept the inevitable, and to recognize what must be recognized, whilst attempting to destroy the indestructible and to associate irreconcilables. The two nations are the two indestructible forces that policy alone makes hostile. They can only live together as nations without an attempt at denationalization or factitious union, and according to the laws of nature and providence. Twenty generations, however, of varied attempts at corruption, intimidation, division, of massacre, torture, or war, seem to have taught our statesmen no lesson. Determined to govern Ireland too much, they have learnt nothing and forgotten everything; but they have strained our most gigantic intellects, swept both nations as with the brands of the Furies, and created a situation of appalling danger.

Given two nations, a large and a little one, parts of one empire, with the seat of empire in the larger country, political science exists to adjust the rights and claims of the two nations and the empire, and not to destroy or ignore either. To maintain that the smaller nationality is irreconcilable with the larger, or with empire, and that the only way is to put down the smaller, is simply to quarrel with facts, to deny nature, and to disestablish politics. Now more than ever we want statesmanship, courage, and ideas, and, above all, the common sense of the universal people, when would-be leaders still challenge the fundamental laws of democracy, and the consensus of universal civilization, denying, first, the right of a considerable nation to govern itself from its own capitol, and next, the possibility of doing what has been done over and over again by other people—to develop and reconcile national and imperial rights and interests in two parliaments and one empire.

Constitutional problems, long since familiar to millions upon millions of our youth and race elsewhere, seem strangely to puzzle over- or under-educated Englishmen at home. The first position, however, that against nationality, one may safely leave to the tender mercies of the English or any other people. We all know what we thought of the rights of Italy, Greece, Hungary, and of the wrongs of Austrian and Turk; and many of us remember the stir there was in England and America when Kossuth declared that if Hungarian liberties were to go down—

"A world in blood shall attend the funeral rites."

Suffice it to say, with President Adams, "there can be no proscription old enough to supersede the law of nature and the grant of God Almighty; Acts of Parliament against the fundamental principles of the British constitution are void;" or with our own John Bright at Limerick, that we believe what every Englishman believes of every country but Ireland, that the government of Ireland should be in accordance with the wishes of the majority of its people, and also that what one Act of Parliament established, another Act could repeal.[1]

It was Burke who said:

"The spirit of nationality is at once the bond and the safeguard of kingdoms; it is something above laws and beyond thrones, the impalpable element, the inner life of States; but anti-nationality is the confusion and downfall of kingdoms; it is a blight and a mildew to the heritage of the people."

We, however, challenge the verdict of the world on this issue in the name also of the universal spirit of humanity, whose chief champion is the British Empire and race, as well as in the name of the coming democratic confederation of all the Britains, the best guarantee of that empire and of that humanity to the world.

As a matter of scientific federal adjustment, we might cite the Constitutions of all the American States and the dicta of all her first statesmen, who, with separate parliaments in every State, built up out of a mass of divers nationalities, in the name of "we the people," both Constitution and nation. The question was well put by Washington, and equally well by Lincoln in his inaugural:

"This relative matter of national power and State rights is no other than the principle of Generality and Locality. Whatever concerns the whole, should be confided to the whole; whatever concerns only the State, should be left exclusively to that State."

From the widest view of the "Philosophy of History," Hegel explains how:

"Each individual national genius is to be treated as only one individual in the process of universal history. The forms which

[1] See "Gladstone's House of Commons," p. 341.

these grades of progress assume are the characteristic national spirits of history; the peculiar tenor of their moral life, of their government, art, religion, and science. To realize these grades is the boundless impulse of the world spirit, the goal of its irresistible urging. For this division into organic members and the full development of each is its idea."

It is therefore but as one of these "grades of boundless impulse and irresistible urging" that the "making of the Irish nation" and of the Britannic Empire now proceed *pari passu* on the right lines laid down by Grattan, Burke, and Fox a century ago. Those who are enemies of the nation are enemies of the empire; but those are the greatest enemies just now of both who cannot see that whilst empire is imperial, "nation" must be national and royal. A nation that comes into an empire can alone come into it as a nation, because it wills to do so, and not because it must. That is the mistake of those who cannot see that the principle of nationality, the only royalty, must cover all.

The sole link of the parliament of Grattan with England was the Crown, and that was then enough; for had the English let them, Irishmen would have been more English than themselves. But with the century the empire has grown and distance has lessened, and the empire, though not the nation, requires closer riveting and stronger links. Still, after the century inaugurated by Pitt, who bought scoundrels, slaughtered patriots, and made the future difficult, Irish nationality once more towers above all its friends and foes—the dominant fact of the situation. With it alone and the English nation, and the empire it can mar or make, we have now to reckon.

"The ocean still protests against separation, and the sea against union." On the one hand, we now cross the sea in four hours instead of twenty-two; and, on the other, we have forced Irish emigration from Canada to the United States, where now nearly two millions of Irish live. But then we have Victoria instead of George III., Gladstone instead of Pitt, and federal ideas have germinated and spread. We hear everywhere of home rule for London, for Wales, for Scotland, and for the counties, and of a real imperial chamber in London relieved of mere titular noblemen, and made ready, as I for one have for eighteen years been urging, for the delegates of empires and of colonies beyond the seas and beneath the setting sun.

The treaty of peace and unity between the two nations, which Grattan negotiated, George III. ratified, and Pitt violated, had, I say, no link of empire but the Crown. But Irish representatives, now led by Parnell, would be far from rejecting such a quota (proportional to the other colonies, nations, and empires to be represented) of imperial federal representation as would put Ireland on a fair federal footing. Ireland must come as a king and as a nation, because in democracies all nations are royal, or she cannot come at all. She is ready so to come, and the English and Scottish nations ask so to receive her. Who, then, is he that would say them nay? Certainly no democratic statesman.

The Colonies cannot come, Ireland ought not to come, into a chamber of mere local self-government or vestry statesmanship. But all that is going to be altered in London; neither Ireland, nor the delegates of our mighty empires beyond the seas, can come as equals and sit down with mere titular sons of their fathers, who represent nothing and are nothing; neither can they come into a chamber where, as Burke said, there would be a mere confused and scuffling bustle of local agency. They will all come, as alone they can come, of their own free royal will. The empire depends on this as well as the nations.

The traitors, then, are those not only to Ireland, but to the whole scheme and scope of Democracy and Federation — of the coming democratic federation of all the

Britains—who look only to the new Irish charter for margin whereon to stamp once more the character of besotted Tory coercionists, or of Whig brutality and littleness.

In 1843 O'Connell brought the entire case on which he relied for repeal before the chief representative body of Ireland, the Dublin Corporation; and his speech, which lasted the greater part of the 25th February, the opening day, is the whole case. Nobody has ever stated it so well, and I insert here a very compressed summary:

"Ireland was fit for legislative independence in position, population, and natural advantages. Five independent kingdoms in Europe possessed less territory or people; and her station on the Atlantic between the old world and the new designed her to be the *entrepôt* of both. She was entitled to legislative independence. The parliament of Ireland was as ancient as that of England, and had sprung out of the natural rights of free men.

"After 1782 her commerce was extended, her manufactures fostered, wages rose, and the value of land increased. During parliamentary independence the use of tea increased 84 per cent. in Ireland, against 45 in England; the use of wine 75 against 22; coffee, 600 per cent. as against 79, and so on the other taxable articles, the use of which measures prosperity. After the union the proportions were reversed.

"He denied, in the name of constitutional law and public faith, that the union was a compact which the Irish Parliament was entitled to make, or which was binding on the Irish people. The ordinary principles of delegated power ruled the case. Locke, the apostle of the revolution of 1688, distinctly declares that 'A legislature cannot transfer the power of making laws into other hands, for, being but a delegated power from the people, they who have it cannot pass it over to others.' They could extinguish themselves, but parliament they could not extinguish."

On the second branch of the proposition, that the compact made by parliament was not binding on the country, O'Connell made out a case of specific fraud and coercion sufficient to invalidate a document before a court of law.

"The union was carried by profligate corruption and naked intimidation. The Irish people were not free agents. The people were prostrate and gagged. Within parliament a majority was bought and paid for; over a million was spent in secret bribes; and a million and a half openly. In the army, navy, customs, patronage was distributed as bribes: £8,000 for a vote, or an office of £2,000 a year. No less than twenty peerages, ten bishoprics, one Chief Justiceship, and six puisne judgeships, were given to men who voted for the union. Twenty-seven counties out of thirty-two petitioned against the union. The petition from County Down was signed by 17,000 persons against, and only 415 for, and so in other counties. There were upwards of 700,000 petitioners against, including the leading men of the nation; those for did not exceed 3,000, some only asking for discussion.

"The union robbed the people of their constitutional right to control the judiciary and executive. It forced them to submit to imperfect representation in the Commons and in corporations, and to see public employments, paid by their money, given to aliens.

"It was said that an Irish parliament would lead to Catholic ascendency. Since the Reformation they had three times been restored to power, and it was admitted by Protestant historians that they had never persecuted a single individual. In an Irish parliament nine-tenths of the peers would be Protestants. Had the Catholics of Ireland shown any indisposition to elect Protestant representatives? Notoriously they had not."

And then came O'Connell's magnificent peroration, with its solid argument as to self-government and prosperity, and its appeal to the interests and imagination :

"Do you know any country submitted to slavery that has not accepted poverty along with it? and do you know any country risen to liberty without prosperity? Look to America, Venice, Switzerland. Look to Belgium, a pitiful province of Holland, now a prosperous nation. Look to Norway, though barren and sterile, which has through a domestic parliament acquired prosperity never before known amongst its hardy population. Ours is a country for man to delight in, whilst her people are foremost in every physical and social quality, temperate, moral, religious, hospitable, and brave. That people shall be what they ought to be. The star of liberty shall beam above them. Self-government and self-legislation shall be revived amongst them. Their allegiance to the throne is unbroken; but their love of liberty is unextinguished and unconquerable."

Fox had declared it to be:

"The most arrogant of all pretensions that we can legislate for Ireland—that we should understand all her local interests better than herself. The sovereignty of the people, that man shall be his own governor, is the fundamental principle of all well-conducted States. To undertake to legislate for persons with whose local interests we must be unacquainted is despotism, not liberty, and the attempt to govern for them was the most audacious which the history of mankind recorded."

And respecting the way to make a strong Ireland and a united empire by a separate legislature, Grattan (January 15, 1800) was still more emphatic:

"After fifteen years, and when the Minister has a great army in Ireland, instead of a Constitution which established peace in Ireland, he revived a principle which produced war in America; namely, that two independent legislatures are incompatible. This was the language of Lord North's sword in the Colonies; this is the language of Mr. Pitt's sword in Ireland; and this doctrine of imperial legislature, which lost America and which Great Britain surrendered to Ireland, takes once more its bloody station in the speeches of the Minister, in defiance of faith, and in contempt of experience. . . . I put this question to my country. Will you fight for a union as you would for a Constitution; for that Lords and that Commons who took away your trade, as for that King, Lords, and Commons who have restored both?

"How came the Irish Parliament with all its borough members in 1779 to demand free trade—in 1782 to demand a free Constitution?

"Because it sat in Ireland, in their own country; because they had a country."

The allegation that Ulster also is a nation is the *reductio ad absurdum* of "nationalities." Ulster was a Presbyterian garrison colony, impropriated and planted by force and confiscation on the native soil. Leaving Belfast out, the Catholics have a majority, and the Nationalists of Ulster have an actual majority in Parliament. A majority in a section has rights, but amongst them no lawyer would include the right to disintegrate the nation. Ulster farmers maintained their rights against landlordism by superior shooting. They were not so loyal and long-suffering as other Irishmen, either to king, landlord, or nation. In Grattan's time they rallied as one man to the national standard, and, as Lecky says, divisions vanished like a dream.

As Pitt's Viceroy wrote him in 1782, the movement that had to be "managed" was "the whole of the country," not only the Church, law, army, merchant, tradesman, manufacturer, farmer, labourer, but "the Catholic, the Dissenter, and the Protestant." But Pitt's policy of division, and the "interesting" interviews his Viceroy had with the chief men of Ulster during the tour undertaken purposely to detach the provinces from the nation, met with some success.

Later on, "superior shooting" has also had a good deal to do with the exuberance of Orange demonstrations, and one effect of Lord Spencer's idea lately of taking police notes of Orange as well as of Nationalist orations, with the story in the sequel, of sacks full of revolvers dropped on the field at a hint of search—these things are instructive as well as comical. When Lord Spencer began to keep Orange magistrates and deputy-lieutenants in order, Orangemen left off teaching Nationalists to take revolvers to their meetings. It is true, as is said at p. 520 of "The Parnell Movement," that "the province of Ulster has, with a characteristic ignorance of Irish affairs, been regarded as a solid mass in favour of English domination.

But in 1798 the most stubborn resistance to the success of the English forces was made in Ulster. Ulster Presbyterians gave to the American Revolution its bravest soldiers. Among them the foundation was laid of the 'United Irishmen,' the most formidable conspiracy against English rule. In more modern times they formed one of the strongest elements of the tenant-right party. At all times in the history of Ulster, the Catholics formed nearly half of the population, and were Nationalist to a man, but the landlords, the boards, the bench, were from the opposite ranks."

The greater number of Ulster Protestants are tolerant and Liberal, many are Nationalists and Home Rulers, or a majority of Home Rulers would not have been returned therefrom. What the intolerant portion fear is not fair Home Rule, but that their own unfair Ulster rule may go out of fashion. We know that Protestants have at all times been on Dublin and other town councils, that Catholic constituencies elect irrespective of creed, that Irish national leaders have been (O'Connell excepted) and are Protestants; whilst no Catholics sit on the Belfast Town Council, and hardly any are yet employed by its Corporation. Many Liberal Presbyterians of Ulster helped the Nationalists at the last election, and with independence the national feeling will naturally obliterate provincial distinctions and differences.

One thing should be said at once, the political unity of the empire never has been in question, and (in this connection) never has been endangered, except by the foes of Irish nationality. Grattan, Fox, and Burke, its boldest advocates, always urged Irish autonomy and imperial unity as one question and interest; nor can they be scientifically stated otherwise. I quote three passages from Burke, one from Grattan, and one from Fox:

".The great trident that was to move the world must be grasped by England alone. Independence of legislature has been granted to Ireland, but no other independence could Great Britain give her without reversing the order of nature. Ireland could not be separated from England; she could not exist without her; she must ever remain under the protection of England, her guardian angel." [1]

"I cannot conceive," said Burke, in 1796, "how a man can be a genuine Englishman without being at the same time a true Irishman. I think the same sentiments ought to be reciprocated on the part of Irishmen, and if possible with much stronger reason. Ireland cannot be separated one moment from England without losing every source of her prosperity, and even hope of her future."

"The whole of the superior, and what I should call imperial politics, ought to have its residence here, and Ireland, locally, civilly, and commercially independent, ought politically to look to Great Britain in all matters of peace or war, and, in a word, with her to live and die." [2]

"To appease and allay the great discontent, I proposed the complete independence of Ireland. The principle was above all . . . to restore that cordial affection between the two countries so eminently requisite to the preservation and prosperity of both. The more Ireland is under the Irish Government, the more will she be bound to British interests." [3]

"I say the growth of Irish demands was the expression of the time, an agreement to establish for ever the free and independent existence of the Irish Parliament, and to preserve for ever the unity of empire, by precluding the introduction of any further constitutional questions affecting the connection founded on the prudent, the profound, the liberal, and the eternal principle of unity of empire and separation of parliament." [4]

Pitt's union did not succeed because it could not succeed. It undid, destroyed, and reversed a right revolution, and set up a union with every element of dissolution and sepa-

---

[1] 1785: Debate on Pitt's resolutions relating to commercial arrangements with Ireland.
[2] Burke, 1797.   [3] Fox, March 23, 1797.   [4] Grattan, 1800.

ration. Witness Hume and Burke in praise of "1782," and Goldwin Smith in condemnation of "1801":

"The revolution of 1688," said Hume, "was accomplished by the first persons in the country in rank and intellect leading the people. Hence it ended in liberty, not confusion. The revolution in Ireland in 1782 was formed in a similar manner."

"The revolution to you," said Burke, "that which most intrinsically and substantially resembled the English revolution of 1688—was the Irish revolution of 1782."

"The incorporation (1707) of the Scotch nation," wrote Goldwin Smith in 1868 to *The Daily News*, "with the English, being conducted by the great Whig statesmen of Anne, has been perfectly successful. The attempt to incorporate the Irish nation with the English and Scotch, conducted on different principles, has failed. The Irish union has missed its port, and, in order to reach it, will have to tack again. The real root is the want of national institutions, of a national capital and life. Dublin is a modern Tara, a metropolis from which the glory has departed. In Ireland we can make no appeal to patriotism, because everything patriotic is rebellious.

"Ulster immigrants were from the Scottish lowlands, Scottish in political and social character. The other three provinces are covered with a mass of population formed out of the wreck of broken Celtic clans, the immemorial enemies of the English government, and who never saw a parliament except as the organ of a foreign oppressor; who lost their only object of political attachment when their chiefs were struck down, and the clan lands confiscated by the strangers' treason law, whose only political ideas are those of clan devotion to a chief, and to each other; whose notions of land tenure belong rather to the clan age of tribal than of individual proprietorship, who are Roman Catholic and Ultramontane in religion, and whose one pervading sentiment is practical hatred of England."

We must now take the great central idea of Irish nationality, and work from it outwards for our policy, remembering always the motto, "The sea protests against union, the ocean protests against separation." We could not work this problem out before, because our people were deceived, our statesmen ignorant, and our king—George III.; because of the minority-garrison Church, and the minority garrison of landlords, of whom three families alone, the Devonshires (Hartingtons), the Beresfords, and the Ponsonbys, were enough at one time to render all right government impossible.

Organization is really a hierarchy, ascending from individuals, communes, municipalities, and counties to nations: "empire" consists of all these united amongst themselves; and, in our case, all preparing for confederation.

But before federation we must found the empire, and before the empire the nations; and we must not mistake local self-government for nationality. I am glad here to quote some profound remarks of the historian Lecky, on Irish nationality:

"One of the most alarming features of Irish disloyalty is its close and evident connection with education. It was long customary to underrate disaffection by ascribing it to transitory causes. The quarter of a century that followed the union was marked by almost perpetual disturbance, but this, it was said, was merely the natural ground-swell.... It was the work of O'Connell, &c., as if the Æolian harp being shattered, men wrote an epitaph on the wind! Public opinion (in Ireland) has palpably deteriorated, and faith in moral force has almost vanished with the failure of his agitation.

"In no other history especially can we investigate more fully the evil consequences which must ensue from disregarding that sentiment of nationality which is at least one of the strongest and most enduring of human passions. This lies at the root of Irish, discontent. Special grievances become formidable only as far as they are connected with it.

"Irish emigration is leavening the new world. Irish administrators under the British Crown are organizing in no small degree the empires or republics of the future. Emigration is multiplying enemies of England throughout the new world. Disloyalty restricts the flow of capital, and the direction of so large an amount of the enthusiasm of the country in opposition to the law, and the diversion of much more into sectarian channels, vitiates and debases political life.

"The three requisites of good government for Ireland are that it should be strong, just, and national. No government will ever command the real affection and loyalty of the people which is not in some degree national, as in Hungary, Switzerland, Belgium. National institutions alone will obtain the confidence of the nation. To give the greatest amount of self-government compatible with the unity and security of the empire should be the aim of every statesman.

"The Irish cared very little on the subject (Disestablishment), but its effects on Protestants have been extremely great. They have been cut loose from their old moorings, and are certainly more disposed than at any period since the union to throw themselves into the general current of Irish sentiment."[1]

That any Irish disloyalty previous to a recognition of her nationality should be used as a presumption of disloyalty after such recognition is forbidden by the precedent of Canada.

Canada, said Mr. Chamberlain, is loyal and friendly to this country; Ireland is not. But, replied the Hon. C. Gavan Duffy, in *The Contemporary Review* for May, to men familiar with the facts, this is the most stringent argument for Mr. Gladstone's proposal. Canada did not get home rule because she was loyal and friendly, but she is loyal and friendly because she got home rule.

"The differences of race and religion have been paraded as barriers to common action, as if the same had not been overcome in Switzerland, Hungary, and Belgium. Is not difference of political sentiments the basis of responsible government? It is precisely because men differ widely in principle that parliamentary government is possible and salutary."

[1] Lecky on "Leaders of Public Opinion in Ireland," preface. 1871.

I venture here to introduce certain invaluable excerpts from Mr. Froude's " English in Ireland : " first, because his book contains the best summary of facts on the ground they cover; second, because those facts are the best vindication of Irish nationality; and third, because they utterly and absolutely nullify all Mr. Froude's assumptions against it. They are also the best illustration of the way in which such very superior persons are apt to cry up authority, and cry down the people.

Messrs. Froude and Lecky both admit the great premiss, nationality, and deny the conclusion, self-government; whilst Mr. Goldwin Smith—who was wont once to belittle the Britannic Empire because the Colonies did not pay, has now taken that empire under his protection—writes to *The Times* to say what large views he; "a Colonist," can take, and shows how little he cares for nationality, self-government, or empire, by belabouring the greatest man now living in the world, for doing all that one man can to make Ireland, and by making Ireland to make the empire.

"Without examining details, the whole of Liberal Europe and America is loud in admiration of the initiative taken by the illustrious statesman," writes M. Emile de Laveleye, in *The Pall Mall Gazette* of May 6th; and on the same date *The Nation*, of New York, thus notices Mr. Goldwin Smith's "indiscretions" in asserting the contrary as to America. *The Nation* must know something about America, and it regrets that the international and omniscient professor has abused his trust. The real sentiments of "the bulk of the Americans" (against Home Rule and Mr. Gladstone) "must have been communicated to him in confidence, with instructions to tell no one, because their open professions are all the other way. To go and blurt it all out is an indiscretion. The only way he can atone for it is to die on the field with Mr. Froude, &c., in conquering the Irish."

Messrs. Froude and Lecky, having amassed with infinite labour an infinitude of facts, miss the mighty generalizations those facts lead to, get lost in their own labyrinths of policy, and fail to master the true perspective of events. Mr. Goldwin Smith wrote in 1868, that what the Irish want is national institutions, the British Government "having missed their port, must tack again;" and ever since he has been walking away from the inevitable inference. Mr. Lecky, too, in 1871, seemed going straight for nationality and its surroundings. Mr. Froude, however, is the most conspicuous offender. He admits that "Ireland was in fact a foreign country; we preferred to assume that she was an integral part of the empire;" that "if the object of our policy was to absorb and extinguish the spirit of Irish nationality, it singularly failed;" that "Grattan had created a nation," &c. He then recounts how, although "two centuries had been allowed the Saxon intruder to win the affections of the native race, the Irish, still oppressed and in rags, were told that if they wanted more than the privilege of sending one of their Protestant masters to Parliament, they must arm." He then turns round, and complains that "the Irish peasant, if set loose, and told to be his own governor, flies at the hand which has unlocked his chain," and that it "was constitutional government which she wanted honesty to use, which plunged her into a deeper abyss of ruin."[1] He clearly explains in the Duke of Portland's words, that "the House of Commons could not yield because to yield to the clamours of the Irish Catholics was the way to make them irresistible and ungovernable; must change the constitution of the House of Commons, and with it overthrow the Church Establishment. The House of Commons was composed largely of members for small boroughs erected purposely to maintain the Protestant ascendency. Common sense and human nature forbad

[1] "The English in Ireland," book v. p. 183.

that these boroughs could survive the change now intended; a Reform Bill might follow, and all the declarations and assurances which might now be given, could not prevent a consequent revolution in Church and State."[1] He sets forth the words of Westmoreland, Viceroy, to Dundas, December 12, 1792, how Catholics and Protestants were to be set by the ears because "every step of conciliating the two descriptions of people that inhabit Ireland, diminishes the probability of that object to be wished—a union with England." He then describes the infernal policy by which Ulster, united in 1782 with the nation for independence, seceded from it, conspired against it, and at last broke the arm and the heart of the Pitt-stirred insurrection, and he finishes with attributing all this mischief to concession, in one of the meanest sentences in the English tongue. "To such an attitude," he says, "had *concession* brought the three million loyal hearts and hands, who in the American war, when the penal laws were at their height, had laid themselves at the feet of the best of kings."

Mr. Froude ends his book by extolling Fitzgibbon (Lord Clare), who, in February, 1789, recommended to the Irish House and nation "one king, one law, one religion," as the one supremely capable man in the Irish House, and gives "one more extract" to be diligently "studied by statesmen," from the speech of this conspicuous Irish traitor against Irish nationality. The passage so extolled is this :

"If we are to pursue faction and folly, it were better that Ireland sink in the sea than to remain attached to England on the terms of our present connection. It has been demanded how are we to be relieved by a union? I answer, we are to be relieved from British and Irish faction. When I look at the

---

[1] Duke of Portland to Lord Fitzwilliam, February 16, 1795, second and secret letter. Froude, "The English in Ireland," book viii. p. 133.

squalid misery of the mass of the Irish people, I am sickened with the rant of Irish dignity and independence. I would elevate Ireland to her proper station in the rank of civilized nations. I would advance her from the degraded post of a mercenary province to the proud station of an integral and governing member of the greatest empire in the world."

Here, then, is a marvellous thing for students—that Mr. Froude, in 1874, believed that the union tends to put down faction; that the union, followed as it immediately was by land laws, which it alone rendered possible, ten times worse than before, has had nothing to do with Irish misery; and that rant about Irish dignity and independence consists not in extolling the union which has presented Ireland with perpetual coercion acts, but in promoting that national self-government which, as Burke, Fox, and Grattan argued, would best unite the empire, and understand the real wants and wishes of the nation. And these are the arguments of a great historian for " the union " !

The volunteers were Ireland's opportunity, the division of interests and factions was England's policy, and their reunion is Ireland's hope and resurrection. That Irish nationality could come to the birth after six hundred years of such birth-throes, and could rise again after eighty-six years of burial, is all the proof possible of her right, short of a miracle; and if any will not believe that, neither would they believe though all the millions Pitt and Castlereagh have murdered, and Froude and Lecky have slandered, rose in battalions from the dead!

About thirty years ago the policy of repentance and compromise began with the Gladstone epoch. The people of England began to grasp the situation and grapple with it; to shake hands with the people of Ireland; to take to heart the mighty words of Burke, Grattan, Fox, and Sheridan, that Irish independence means imperial unity;

to believe that you can only make the British Empire by making the Irish nation; and to see that *both nations*—the Irish as the English—have commissioned the great man of the epoch, William Ewart Gladstone, and will follow him.

Gladstone now demands a mandate, and calls on the English nation to play, not the little provincial game of party, but the high, imperial, manly game of politics. We may do this, because we will; but if not, we shall do it because we must. No longer can "I dare not wait upon I would." We have lost one hundred years, and the questions of nationality and empire will return to-day, to-morrow, and for ever, until they are united by conciliation, statesmanship, and common sense.

It is time that the mighty armies of English thinkers, and of the English people, now united, should arise under Gladstone's banner, and wrest the rod of rule and empire from the cut-throats of both—from the "here-we-are-agains" and "happy-go-luckies" of the sections. It is time that the preponderating power of this empire should shatter the statesmanship of chaos, thimblerigging, and despair, which calls separation union, and union separation, and pretends that to do justice and conciliate Ireland is to dismember the empire.

> "England has built her everlasting mansion
> Upon the beached verge of the salt flood."

We are the universal Venice, and all the waters of the world our streets and thoroughfares! If justice and conciliation do not save us, their absence will help to sink us. If our policy does not unite us with Ireland, it will separate us from her. The policy which secures alongside us an open back-door of intrigue for the Bismarcks of the world, which keeps open on our flank the eternal vengeful sore of Ireland, ceases now to be regarded as a mark of statesmanship or sense. There are now two millions too many voters for that!

The sum of the matter is that each nation must preserve what is essential to itself—Ireland, her nationality; England, such control over Ireland as will prevent her from being used by enemies of England, or the empire, and as will secure her as one of the first-fruits of Federation. Self-development and preservation are the first law of politics.

I endeavour shortly to show :
1. How Ireland became a nation and got Home Rule.
2. How that worked.
3. How it was taken away.
4. What followed Pitt's union, and has got to follow.

IRELAND A NATION.

"It is voted upon question *nullo contradicente*, that the subjects of this, His Majesty's kingdom, are a free people, and to be governed only according to the common law of England, and statutes made and established in this kingdom, of Ireland, and according to the lawful customs used in the same."— *Irish Commons Journal*, July 26, 1641.

"His Majesty, being concerned to find that discontents and jealousies are prevailing amongst his loyal subjects in Ireland, upon matters of great weight and importance, earnestly recommends to this house to take the same into their most serious consideration, in order to such a final adjustment as may give mutual satisfaction to both kingdoms."—*G. R., Royal Message to English Commons*, 1782.

Similar Royal Message to Irish House through the Duke of Portland, April 16, 1782.

"His Majesty commands me to assure you of his disposition to give his assent to Acts to prevent the suppression of Bills in the Privy Council of this kingdom, and the alteration of them anywhere; and to limit the duration of the Act for the better regulation of His Majesty's forces in this kingdom to the term of two years."—*Viceroy to Irish House*, May 27, 1782.

Statute 6 Geo. I., c. 5, which declared the dependency of Ireland, was repealed April, 1782.

"That the said right claimed by the people of Ireland to be bound only by laws enacted by His Majesty, and the parliament of that kingdom in all cases whatever, and to have all actions, &c., decided in His Majesty's court therein finally, and without appeal from thence, . . . shall be, and it is hereby declared to be established and ascertained for ever, and shall at no time hereafter be questioned or questionable."—*Statute* 23 *Geo. III.*, c. 28, 1783.

"If any man entertained gloomy ideas, look at the Irish Addresses. The Irish people and parliament were filled with the most earnest desire to support England, to have the same enemy and the same friend; in a word, to stand or fall with England. Look forward to that happy period when Ireland . . . should become a powerful country; then might England look for powerful assistance in seamen to man her fleet, and soldiers to fight her battles. England renouncing all right to legislate for Ireland, the latter would cordially support the former as a friend whom she loved; if this country, on the one hand, was to assume the power of making laws for Ireland, she must only make an enemy instead of a friend. The Irish desired nothing more ardently than proper grounds for being most cordially united to England; and he was sure they would be attached to this country, even to bigotry."—Fox, 1782. Hansard, v. 23, pp. 27, 28, " Motion to repeal 6 Geo. I."

" How came the Irish Parliament with all its borough members in 1779 to demand Free Trade, in 1782 to demand a free constitution? Because it *sat in Ireland*, in their own country; because they had a country. But the market of *St. Stephen opened*. These gentlemen of the empire, absent from one country and unelected by the other, suspended between both and belonging to neither, . . . will be adventurers dressed and sold in the shrouds and graveclothes of the Irish Parliament, and playing for hire their tricks on her tomb, the images of degradation and the representatives of nothing."—GRATTAN, January 15, 1800. *Speeches*, v. 3, pp. 364, 365.

" But for the union," said Daniel O'Connell, reviewing these events in 1843,[1] "we should have been emancipated by our Protestant fellow-countrymen long before. In 1778 they restored the Catholics to the equal enjoyment of all property they then held, and enabled them to acquire long terms for years in lands. In 1782, the Irish Protestants restored the Catholics to the capacity of acquiring every species of freehold property, and to enjoy it equally with Protestants. In 1792-3 the learned professions were to a certain extent opened to Catholics—the grand jury box, the magistracy, partial rank in the army, were all conceded by the Irish Protestants to their Catholic fellow-countrymen. But, greatest of all, the elective franchise was restored. Under these circumstances, but for the union, full and complete emancipation would have been conceded before 1803."

[1] Discussion in Dublin Corporation on repeal of the union.

IRELAND A NATION.

CHAPTER II.

1782.

IRELAND A NATION.

Swift, Molyneux, Flood, Grattan, Fox, Burke, Charlemont, and the Volunteers.

"It was an agreement to establish for ever the free and independent existence of the Irish Parliament, and to preserve for ever the unity of empire, by precluding then and for all times to come, the introduction of any further constitutional questions affecting the connection which was to rest under solemn covenant, inviolable, impregnable, and invincible, to the intrigue or ambition of either country—founded on the prudent, the profound, the liberal and the eternal principle of unity of empire and separation of parliament. . . .

"That was the age of the repeal of the penal code, of the Habeas Corpus Act. The army was made parliamentary; the revenues annual; trade became free; the power of the Irish Parliament who could before only originate petitions, was restored in full, complete, and exclusive authority. . . .

"I affirm that the blessings procured by the Irish Parliament in the last twenty years are greater than all the blessings afforded by British Parliaments to Ireland for the last century, greater even than the mischiefs inflicted on Ireland by the British Parliament."—GRATTAN.

THE present object not being so much to write history as to bring into one purview the two processes of the division and conquest of Ireland by England, followed and reversed by the gradual reunion of all Irish forces and parties in order to the final conquest of her liberties, we need pass but lightly over her story until we come to the times of Swift, Flood, and Grattan, the makers of the Irish nation, and of Pitt and Castlereagh, its would-be destroyers. Suffice it therefore to say, that Irish history has for our purposes three substantial epochs — first, from Henry II. and his charter from the Pope to 1782, when Ireland obtained her independence; the second, from 1782 to 1801, the period of nominal independence, ended by corruption, massacre, and prostration; and the third, from 1801, the date of nominal union and onwards, to the Gladstone epoch.

There is no doubt, as Dr. Johnson said, "Ireland was the school of the West, the great habitation of sanctity and learning;" or even, as Guizot explains, that "of all the countries of the West Ireland was, for a long time, that in which alone learning was supported, and throve amid the general overthrow of Europe."

The early history of Ireland is indeed "lost in the mists of antiquity," but in 1417 at the Council of Constance, England obtained the precedence over France on account of the greater antiquity of Ireland; and the argument was taken from the authority of Albertus Magnus and Bartholomæus, who state that in the division of the world, Europe was subdivided into four great kingdoms — Rome, Constantinople, Ireland, and Spain.

Irish records have mostly been mutilated or destroyed, but in Rymer's Fœdera is a writ to convene an Irish Parliament in 38th Henry III., A.D. 1253; a statute of that year is still extant on the roll. There is also an Act of the Parliament of Edward I., the list of whose members appears in the history of Sir Richard Cox; and Sir Richard Bolton, the chief Baron, published an edition of Irish Statutes in 1621.

In the British Museum is a work entitled, "Proceedings of the Parliament in Ireland, beginning March 25, 1689," in which Acts were passed, James being present and supporting them, that gave to Ireland a free and independent Constitution, destroyed the British supremacy, repealed Poyning's law of 1494, abolished appeals to England, and established liberty of conscience.

In the time of Edward I. the Irish demanded the benefits of British law, and in the time of Charles, an independent parliament. Sir John Perrot, President of Munster in the time of Elizabeth, says, " They will do more at the command of their governor, whom they repute and have found just, than by the constraint of any power."

Burke said that:

"Ireland, before the English conquest, had no parliament. But we have all the reason in the world to be assured that a form of parliament such as England then enjoyed, she instantly communicated to Ireland. This benefit I confess was not at first extended to all Ireland, and this was the true cause why Ireland was five hundred years in subduing; and after the vain project of a military government attempted in the reign of Queen Elizabeth, it was soon discovered that nothing could make that country English in civility and allegiance but your laws and your forms of legislature. It was not English arms, but the English Constitution, that conquered Ireland. From that time, Ireland has ever had a general parliament. This has made Ireland the great and flourishing kingdom that it is, and rendered her a principal part of our strength and ornament." [1]

And Flood [2] maintained that Ireland had a parliamentary Constitution the same as that of England, an hereditary peerage invested with final judicature, and, before the union, a franchise exactly the same as England, "above three hundred years before any colony in America had a name."

No one can read Irish history, which is nothing but the harrowing of the Irish, without harrowing his own soul. For details with full authorities, it is best to refer the reader who wants them to Daniel O'Connell's little book,

[1] March 22, 1775, Hansard.   [2] See Irish Debates, vi. p. 422.

dated February 1, 1843, and addressed to the Queen.[1] I give here only several short extracts:

"After Elizabeth's wholesale massacres and deliberately created famine, no spectacle was more frequent in the ditches of the towns, and especially in wasted countries, than to see multitudes of these poor Irish dead, with their mouths all coloured green by eating nettles, docks, and all things they could rend above ground. Mark, illustrious lady, dead, dead in multitudes and none to bury. This was the consummation of the subjugation of the Irish, after a contest of 400 years. . . .

"During the 440 years between the commencement of the English dominion in 1172 and its completion in 1612, the Irish were known only as the 'Irish enemies' in royal proclamation, Charters, and Acts of Parliament. It was their legal and technical description. During that time any person of English descent might murder Irish with impunity. If the Irishman had made legal submission, his murder was punishable by a small fine, not for the moral crime of murdering a man, but for depriving the State of a servant. . . .

"The second period of 13 years was from 1612 to 1625, and in it Irish and English were amalgamated for the purpose of enduring spoil and oppression under the name of Catholics. The entire of Ulster was confiscated, the natives executed or slaughtered, the remnant driven to mountain or bay. Their places were filled with Scotch aliens in blood and religion. . . .

"From 1625 to 1660 sat the commission to inquire into defective titles. Charles I. claimed the estates of the Irish in three provinces. Strafford bribed the judges with 4s. in the £ value. . . .

"From 1660 to 1692 the chief events were the taking by the Duke of York, afterwards James II., of 80,000 acres belonging to Irish Catholics; and the Treaty of Limerick. The Irish army, 30,000 strong, had driven William III. from Limerick. In that war, women bled and fought, and conquered. The treaty restored the Irish nation to England, in consideration of protection of property and liberty, especially of religion."

From 1692 to 1778 that treaty was carried out by the

[1] Duffy, Dublin and London.

utter proscription of the property, the education, the personal rights, and the religion of all Irish Catholics. O'Connell occupies five pages in the mere summary.

"In 1792 Republicanism was eagerly caught up amongst the Protestants, and especially among the Presbyterian population of the north. Belfast was its warmest focus. Government set itself to conciliate Catholics, and separate them from the republican party of Ulster, as it has since often tried to separate Ulster from Ireland."

In 1155, Henry II. sought permission of Pope Hadrian IV. to enter Ireland, in order, as he put it, to "enlarge the bounds of the Church, to restrain the progress of vices, to correct the manners of the people, to plant virtue among them, and to increase the Christian religion." This was complied with on the terms that Henry should compel every Irish family to pay a carolus to the Pope, and that he should hold the island as the Pope's fief.

In 1465 was passed the celebrated Head Act; by which any Irish found "going or coming, having no faithful man of good name and fame in their company in English apparell," it was lawful to kill, cut off heads, and put it on spear in castle of Trim; and levy by his own hand, as his reward, of every man with one ploughland in the barony, 2d., of half of one ploughland, 1d., some others were to pay ½d.

Henry VII. preserved the Irish Parliament, but destroyed its independence.

He sent Sir Edward Poyning to Ireland as his deputy, and in 1494 convened a parliament, and passed what has since been called Poyning's Act, which enacted that there should be no parliament unless the Lieutenant and Council there certify under the Great Seal the causes and consideration, &c.; also, that no legislation was valid unless approved by the king and the English Council under the Great Seal of England. Thus the approval of the Irish Council, and that of the English Privy Council, was made necessary before Acts could be even submitted to the Irish Parliament; and the Irish Constitution consisted of the King, the Irish Lords and Commons, the Irish Lieutenant and Council, and the English Privy Council.

Before 1542 English kings were only lords of Ireland, but the "identity and inseparability of the Crown of the two countries" was then enacted, and that "kings of England be always kings of this land of Ireland."

In 1541 the first Irish National Parliament was convened by Henry VIII., Irish as well as English lords being summoned.

Queen Mary granted vast tracts to English immigrants who could hold against the Irish; the latter being driven out and exterminated, and two counties added to the "English pale."

In 1609-12, under James I. (who made forty nominee boroughs, and on remonstrance said, "Suppose I had made four hundred, the more the merrier!"), Ulster was replanted by Scotch and English Protestants; 511,405 acres being cleared, and the natives exterminated.

In 1688 was the contest with the English parliamentary forces, in which 200,000 Irish are said to have perished. Mr. J. S. Mill states that:

"The whole land of the island had been confiscated three times over. Part had been taken to enrich powerful Englishmen and their Irish adherents; part to form the endowment of a hostile hierarchy; the rest had been given away to English and Scotch colonists, who held, and were intended to hold it, as a garrison against the Irish. The manufactures, except the linen, which was chiefly carried on by these colonists, were deliberately crushed, for the avowed purpose of making more room for those of England. The vast majority of the native Irish, all Roman Catholics, were in violation of the faith pledged to the Catholic army at Limerick, despoiled of all their political and most of their civil rights, and left in existence only to plough and dig."[1]

---

[1] See "England and Ireland," 1868. Longmans.

Under the Celtic tenure of gavelkind, a chief was only joint owner with the clan; by the change English statesmen at last accomplished, the chief became absolute proprietor, and in case of attainder, forfeited to the Crown, not a life interest only, but the estate. In good time three-fourths of the soil of Ireland was thus confiscated to the Crown. The sept, from joint owners of the tribal lands, became mere tenants at will, though their title was better than that of Elizabeth to the throne, and tenants at will they have mostly remained to this day.

In Lord Clare's speech, February 10, 1800, in favour of union, he said that "7,800,000 acres of land were set out under Act of Charles II., nearly to the total exclusion of the old inhabitants;" and one of the best-known remarks of Lord Clare is that "the whole power and property of the country has been conferred by successive monarchs of England upon an English colony, composed of three sets of adventurers, who poured into this country at the termination of three successive rebellions—confiscation is their common title."

"In 1698, when the measure for destroying the Irish wool trade was under deliberation, Molyneux, one of the members of Trinity College, an eminent man of science, and the ingenious friend mentioned by Locke in his essay, published his famous case of Ireland. He maintained that the parliament of Ireland had naturally and anciently all the prerogatives in Ireland which the English Parliament had in England, and that the subservience to which it had been reduced was the result of usurpation. His arguments were chiefly historical, and were those which were afterwards maintained by Flood and Grattan, and which eventually triumphed in 1782. By order of the English Parliament his book was burnt by the common hangman."[1]

The Treaty of Limerick, October 3, 1691, guaranteed to the Catholics to retain such estates as they possessed before James II. came to the throne, and to enjoy their

[1] Lecky on Swift, p. 43. 1871 Edition.

religion as they had under Charles II. But when the flower of the Irish army had withdrawn to France, and the remnant could be hanged without ceremony, the concession began to look inordinate.

At the time of the Reformation, Ireland was the only northern country in which the reformed truth never made way. Elizabeth, the great representative of Protestantism, was less anxious to propagate it than to destroy Irish nationality. Cromwell followed; and the last great Protestant, William III., is identified with the destruction of Irish trade, and with the broken Treaty of Limerick, which had guaranteed Catholic privileges as in the reign of Charles II.

"The beginning of the Irish Penal Code was a law passed in 1691 by the English Parliament for excluding all Catholics from the Irish one;" but, adds Lecky, "the spirit in which Ireland was systematically governed in the early part of the eighteenth century was well illustrated by the speech of the Lords Justices to the Parliament in 1715: 'We must recommend to you in the present conjuncture such unanimity as may once more put an end to all other distinctions in Ireland than that of Protestant and Papist.'"

Burke described the code as

"Well digested and well described in all its parts, a machine of wise and elaborate contrivance, and as well fitted for the oppression, impoverishment, and degradation of a people, and the debasement in them of human nature itself, as any that ever proceeded from the perverted ingenuity of man."

Yet Arthur Young asserts that the proportion of Catholics had not diminished. It was stated in Parliament that only 4,055 had conformed in seventy-one years, and according to Lecky, "the poorer classes emerged from the long ordeal penetrated with an attachment to their religion almost unparalleled in Europe."

In 1703 the Irish Parliament petitioned for a union, but their overtures were rejected by the queen's ministers.

The Irish idea seems to have been that the union would have brought more equality and material advantages; but Mr. Froude says:

"The offered union was thrown away in the meanest and basest spirit of commercial jealousy. Those responsible persuaded themselves that the union would make Ireland rich, and that England's interest was to keep her poor. Opportunities occur in the affairs of nations which, if allowed to pass, occur no more."[1]

In 1720 Jonathan Swift published anonymously an admirable pamphlet on Irish manufactures, in which he urged the people to meet restrictions on their trade by burning everything that came from England "except the coal;" concluding by an earnest appeal to landlords to lighten rents.

Then came his famous Drapiers letters against Wood's patent half-pence, the patent being granted by the influence of the king's mistress, who was to receive a large share of the profits. It was the fourth letter which turned the agitation into the national channel. Swift defined boldly the limits of prerogative, asserted the independence of Ireland, and the essential nullity of measures without the sanction of the Irish legislature. He avowed his entire adherence to the doctrine of Molyneux, and asserted that Ireland was rightfully a free nation. This letter was sustained by other pamphlets, and by ballads sung in the streets, and brought the agitation to the highest pitch. Walpole was compelled to yield and withdraw the patent. The age of Grattan and O'Connell had begun. Afterwards, in 1727, Swift published his "Short View of the State of Ireland." When Walpole talked of having him arrested, he was asked if he had ten thousand men to spare. When Primate Boulter charged Swift with exciting the people, he retorted, "If I were only to lift my finger you would be torn to pieces."

[1] "The English in Ireland," book ii. pp. 303, 304.

Swift first taught the Irish people to rely upon themselves. The cause of free trade and legislative independence never again passed out of their minds, and 1782 was the development of his policy.

When occasion arose in 1757 for the more direct assertion of the national idea, the fruits of Swift's and others' teaching at once became apparent in the fury to which Dublin was lashed by the mere rumour, put forth by the English Whigs, of a union with Ireland; and when, in 1767, the Octennial Bill was transmitted and became law, the sixteen months made to elapse between the dissolution of the old parliament (elected for the life of the king) and the meeting of the new were employed by the Viceroy in influencing the latter. The new Irish Parliament, however, could not be bribed to allow the English Council to originate money bills, and the Viceroy postponed the meeting of parliament by a series of prorogations until 1771, when lavish corruption by money and honours secured a majority. That parliament was dissolved because it rejected a money bill altered in the Privy Council, and with the next parliament in 1777 came the patriotic Militia Bill for national defence, and the volunteers.

Ireland then, having an army at her back, turned her attention resolutely to Free Trade. It was broached in the English Commons in 1779, and in the Irish House by amendment on the address, that Free Trade alone could save the nation from ruin. "Free Trade or ———," was labelled on the volunteer cannon. An amendment was carried to vote supplies for only six months, in November; and in February, 1780, Government yielded as to the Irish right to export woollens, and to trade with the British Colonies. But as it became evident that only a free parliament could secure a free trade, Henry Grattan moved in April that "the King, Lords, and Commons of Ireland are alone competent to enact laws to bind Ireland." Both parties exactly understood the situation. The

Mutiny Bill for six months was sent to England as usual. The Privy Council made it perpetual, and a purchased majority in the Irish Commons passed it. The issue now was absolutely clear. Bribery had disposed of parliament. Force and fraud were to be tried with the volunteers and the nation, and in twenty years force and fraud prevailed.

"A majority in the House of Commons," said Froude,[1] "was at this time, 1753, returned by four great families, the Fitzgeralds of Kildare, the Boyles, the Ponsonbys, and the Beresfords—the political sovereigns of Ireland. The government was carried on by their assistance, and they received in return the patronage of the State. The Viceroy understood the meaning of the vote. Patriot orators were silenced by promotion. Opposition to England's initiation of money bills was suspended till the great families were again hungry, and fresh expectants of promotion were in a position to be troublesome."

Flood entered parliament in 1759, when it was very largely corrupt and subservient, and his eloquence and position soon made him the leader of a party to abridge the corrupt influence of the Government, and to establish the independence of parliament.

According to Edmund Burke's "Tracts on the Popery Laws" the lands of Papists were divided between their male children, and every child might compel his popish father to disclose property, and immediately to set apart a third to the child. Catholic families were thus reduced to impotence in William's reign. Catholics could not buy land, although they might get a long lease of fifty acres of bog with half an acre to build a house on. Under this head of the acquisition of property the law met them on every road of industry. Only Established Churchmen could enter the Universities. Popish schoolmasters were proscribed. It was felony to teach in a private house, and outlawry to go abroad for education. A Roman Catholic

[1] "The English in Ireland," book v. pp. 5, 6.

could hold no office of trust or profit, no vote, no corporate privilege, no gun, could not be a barrister or solicitor. There was, said Burke, "universal, unqualified, unlimited proscription."

A statute was fabricated in 1699 by which saying mass was forged into a crime punishable with perpetual imprisonment. Lord Chancellor Bowes and Chief Justice Robinson stated, that "the law does not suppose any such person to exist as an Irish Roman Catholic." The first object was to create a class tyranny and a religious tyranny. The people acquired the vices of slaves, and were educated through generations into hostility to law, and taught to look for redress to illegal violence or secret combinations. The second object of the penal laws was to reduce Catholics to extreme and brutal ignorance. The ownership of land producing loyalty, Government sought to make Protestants landlords and Catholics their tenants. Hence class hatred, religious hatred, the vices of slaves, and the necessities of conspirators. Sir G. C. Lewis's " Local Disturbances in Ireland," published in 1836, describes the combinations of peasantry to shake off their burdens. As a Catholic landlord would have become the natural political leader of his Catholic tenants, and would have neutralized the hatred of his co-equals, both contingencies were avoided by law. But this desperation of Protestantism was carried further still (as is explained by Lecky), for every marriage by a Catholic priest between a Catholic and a Protestant was made null and void, and the priest who officiated was hung. Sydney Smith, writing as Peter Plymley, declared :

"There was an universal agreement to continue every species of internal persecution; to deny at home every right, to pummel the Dissenters, and to treat the Catholics of Ireland as though their tongues were mute, their heels cloven, their nature brutal, and their subjugation providential."

As Burke wrote in 1782, "they," the English usurpers,

"had already almost gone through every contrivance which could waste the vigour of the country; but they produced the shocking Act about marriages which tended to finish the scheme for making the people not only two distinct parties for ever, but two distinct species in the same land." And in 1795 he laments the impolicy of those "two hundred years, dreadfully spent in experiments to force that people to change the form of their religion. The Catholics form the great body of the lower ranks of your country, and no small part of those classes of the middling that come nearest to them. The seduction of that part of mankind from the principles of religion, morality, subordination, and social order is the great object of the Jacobins." The Catholic religion was then, argued Burke, "the most effective barrier, if not the sole barrier, against Jacobinism. You have now your choice—for full four-fifths of your people—of the Catholic religion or Jacobinism."

"As late as Chesterfield's Viceroyalty (1747), though legitimate discontent had been often expressed in the House of Commons, there had been little systematic opposition to the English connection. So long as a combination with the Catholics against English rule was undreamt of, an Irish Protestant patriot was conscious at bottom that he could not maintain himself without England's help. So long as his Protestantism lasted as a real principle, he endured the injuries of his country as a lighter evil than compromise with his old enemy. As the century waned, community of injury created a sympathy of resentment. The steady increase of Irish misery formed a contrast every year more marked with the growing splendour of England; and if material progress was to be the chief aim, there was no conceivable reason why Ireland, Protestant or Catholic, should be denied a share in it." [1]

The reign of George III. however comprises the rise and fall of the Irish nation. He began by turning out

---

[1] See Froude, "The English in Ireland," book iv. pp. 605, 606.

Lord Chatham and bringing in Lord Bute. His principle was absolute power, and his practice was to choose ministers for their capacity for failure. The empire was lost when he was in his senses; its only chance was when he was out of them. After four coalitions, he was beaten out of Europe. Lord North lost him America; Pitt lost him Europe; had he lived, Percival would have lost him England. It was saved by Wellington, an Irishman. When the Irish offered the Crown to the Duke of Lorraine in the time of Charles I., and when they sought French support in 1797, they committed an irretrievable error, which latter had Grattan's utmost opposition, but they had to fight against slavery.

From 1766 to 1820, Burke in the English, or Grattan in the Irish or English Parliaments maintained the people's cause, and the Irish came to their standard.

In June, 1776, we find Arthur Young writing of his twenty-two hours' trip from Holyhead to Dublin:

"There is very good society in Dublin in a parliament winter, two gentleman's clubs, and an unsuccessful attempt at Italian opera. I often frequented the gallery of the House of Commons. Mr. Grattan (and others) are reckoned high among the Irish orators. I heard many very eloquent speeches, but I cannot say they struck me like the exertion of the abilities of Irishmen in the English House of Commons, owing perhaps to the reflection both on the *speaker* and *auditor*, that the Attorney-General of England, with a dash of his pen, can reverse, alter, or entirely do away the matured result of all the eloquence and all the abilities of this whole Assembly."

In 1778 came the first fruits of the growing national unity, the Act of 1704 was annulled, and Catholics might be granted leases for 999 years. They also conquered free trade with the Colonies.

In 1779 the religious test was loosened, and it became possible for Catholics to be official. England was afraid of losing Ireland, and Protestants feared a Catholic rising. Concession after concession was extorted by Grattan.

Grattan first moved for parliaments of seven years, which the English, who then wanted 3,000 more men, granted by altering to eight years. In 1775 the echoes of Bunker's Hill aroused anew the feelings of Irish nationality. In 1778 there was an enrolled army of volunteers of at least 150,000, officered by the gentry of the country; and Catholics who could not be enrolled paid for the muskets of those who could. As the Irish Parliament alone could raise Irish revenue, that was made a lever of concession.

On the despatch of 4,000 Irish troops to America, and the futile demand of the Mayor of Belfast for a garrison against the French, there "arose," says Lecky, on Flood (p. 80), "one of those movements of enthusiasm that occur two or three times in the history of a nation. The cry to arms passed through all the land, and was responded to by all parties and creeds. Beginning among the Protestants of the North, the movement soon spread, though in a less degree, to other parts of the island, and the war of religions and of castes that had so long divided the people vanished as a dream. They rose to defend their country from the invasion of a foreign army, and from the encroachments of an alien legislature. Conspicuous among their colonels was Flood; and there too was he before whose genius all other Irishmen had begun to pale —the patriot of unsullied purity, the statesman who could fire a nation by his enthusiasm and restrain it by his wisdom, the orator whose burning sentences became the very proverbs of freedom—Henry Grattan."

"England," writes Froude, "had sown with poison weeds the draggled island which lay in the rear of her imperial domain. The crop [1] had sprung up and ripened, and now (1776) the harvest was

[1] "The English in Ireland," book vi. p. 189.

to be gathered. England had discharged her sovereign duties to Ireland by leaving her to anarchy masked behind a caricature of the forms of her own Constitution. With an insolent mockery she had refused her request for incorporation in the empire. She had left her the name of a separate kingdom and a separate nationality as her excuse for withholding from her equal rights. The nationality was to become a thorn in England's side. The Irish Parliament became the arena for the partition of the spoil. The English Cabinet retained the pension list for corruption, and the high offices of State as sinecures. Public interests went to ruin. The harbour defences crumbled and disappeared, the military stores were stolen." [1]

"'Townshend and Harcourt had broken the power of the great nobles by bribery, and had taught independent members that the service of the Castle was a safer road to fortune than the service of the Leinsters and Ponsonbys. The established communion had divided Protestantism in two, and had ostracised the most energetic section of it. It drove the Presbyterians into republicanism and disaffection. High offices in the Church were the most effective instruments of political influence and party service. England had forced Ireland into a contraband trade which enlisted half her population in organized resistance to the law. By definite acts of unjust legislation they were forcing the entire people to abandon themselves to the potato, and to sit down to brood over their wrongs in a paralysis of anger and despair." [2]

Every sound and honourable mind in Ireland was now convinced of the necessity of a change, and a knot of gentlemen remained at home whose abilities and character would anywhere have marked them for distinction. Grattan became the voice of his people, and on February 7, 1778, moved an address to the Crown, which was lost, 143 to 66. War had now been declared against France; the country professed its willingness to provide for its own defence, either by volunteer corps or militia; Parliament preferred the volunteers, and the Viceroy was of the same opinion. The cost of militia would fall on the treasury, which was

[1] " The English in Ireland," book vi. pp. 190, 191.   [2] Ibid. p. 198.

empty; and if the lords and gentlemen of Ireland were willing to raise independent companies at their own expense, it would be a pity to reject their liberality.[1] Lord North and the Viceroy had determined that Dissenters' disabilities should be maintained to punish the Presbyterians for their American tendencies.[2] The Irish grand juries represented that the fields and highways were filled with crowds of wretched beings half naked and starving. They besought the king to procure them leave to export and sell at least the coarse frieze blankets and flannels which the peasant's wives and children produced in their cabins. Eloquence and entreaty were alike in vain.[3]

When in 1779 the House went in a body to present their Free Trade petition to the Lord-Lieutenant, the volunteers lined the road and presented arms to them as they passed. Lecky says:

"England could scarcely have resisted an organized body of more than 100,000 soldiers commanded by the men of most property and influence in the country, and supported by the enthusiasm of the nation. I venture to think that the probabilities were, on the whole, in favour of the peaceful dispersion of the force when its work had been accomplished."[4]

Ireland was allowed free export of all her productions except woollens — the great clandestine trade that had been the chief support of the spinners and weavers; and Ireland, now desperate and determined, and treading ominously in the steps of America, resolved, as had been recommended by Swift, to exclude from the Irish market every article of British manufacture.

Meanwhile Ireland was arming. The movement spread as if the whole country had a purpose. The session was to open on October 12, 1779, and Grattan moved "that it was not by temporary expedients, but by a free export,

---

[1] "The English in Ireland," book vi. p. 211.   [2] Ibid. p. 217.
[3] Ibid. p. 222.   [4] "Flood's Life," pp. 95-7.

that the nation was to be saved," which amendment was carried unanimously.[1]

"If the expectations of this kingdom are not received with lenity," wrote the fluttered imbecile, the Viceroy, "'every species of disorder may be apprehended;' but no relief coming, Grattan's motion against new taxes was carried 170 to 47; and when supplies were asked for two years, as usual an amendment passed, 138 to 100, for a six months' money bill.[2] . . . This short money bill," says Froude, "opened the eyes of ministers at last, and, in December, 1779, the repeal of the restriction Acts was proposed on the spot, and swept through the House with extraordinary spirit."[3]

On April 19, 1780, Grattan moved the Irish declaration of rights:

"1. The king, with the consent of the Parliament of Ireland, was alone competent to enact laws to bind Ireland.

"2. Great Britain and Ireland were indissolubly united, but only under the tie of a common sovereign."

On an appeal to Irish generosity the House adjourned without a division.

On November 13, 1781, Grattan's motion to repeal the Mutiny Bill was lost by a large majority.

"What was the consequence"—of their policy attacking Irish interest, and yet hoping to maintain imperial unity? argued Burke, in his great Bristol speech of 1780, made to defend against Bristol merchants his vote against the destruction of Irish trade. "Ireland was in a flame, 40,000 men were raised and disciplined without commission from the Crown. Two illegal armies were seen with banners displayed at the same time and in the same country. They demanded freedom of trade with arms in their hands. The British Parliament made a universal surrender. A sudden light broke in upon us all through the yawning chasms of our ruin."

[1] Froude's "The English in Ireland," book vi. p. 239.
[2] Ibid. p. 244.
[3] Ibid. p. 247.

"I deny," said Sydney Smith, writing as Peter Plymley in 1808, "I deny that any voluntary concession was ever made by England to Ireland. Ask Lord Auckland if he remembers the fatal consequences of trifling with such a people as the Irish. When Ireland demanded rights with the voice of 60,000 armed men, they were granted with every mark of consternation. Ask Lord Auckland if he has forgotten that memorable evening when, as secretary to the Lord-Lieutenant, he came down to the House, booted and mantled, about to set off for Ireland that night, and declared before God if he did not carry with him a compliance with all their demands Ireland was for ever lost to this country."

In 1780, at a meeting of Dublin Volunteers, it had been resolved: "That the King, Lords, and Commons of Ireland only are competent to make laws binding on this realm, and that we will not obey any others."

Before 1782, the principles of the Irish revolution had extended throughout all parts of the kingdom; the volunteers had augmented nearly to 80,000 men, and later to 100,000; the representatives of 143 corps had, in February, assembled in Dungannon, and passed at that celebrated convention resolutions of which the three most essential were:

"That a claim of any body of men other than the King, Lords, and Commons of Ireland, to make laws to bind this kingdom, is unconstitutional, illegal, and a grievance.

"That the powers exercised by the Privy Council of both kingdoms, under, or under colour or pretence of, the law of Poyning are unconstitutional and a grievance.

"That a Mutiny Bill not limited in point of duration from session to session is unconstitutional and a grievance."

To these Grattan added the following, in order to draw all parties and sects into the movement:

"Resolved, That we hold the right of private judgment in matters of religion to be equally sacred in others as in ourselves; that we rejoice in the relaxation of the penal laws against our

Roman Catholic fellow-subjects, and that we conceive the measure to be fraught with the happiest consequences to the union and prosperity of the inhabitants of Ireland."

These resolutions were universally made known and adopted in Ireland.

Flood was not sensible of the importance of concessions to the Catholics, who had at that time (as Lecky, in his "Irish Leaders," explains) neither education, leaders, nor ambition, and were perfectly peaceful, and indeed quiescent, and the process of emancipation would probably have been carried out silently and tranquilly. The most obnoxious of the penal laws had already been repealed, and Lecky adds the following remarks on Grattan's resolution :

"It is scarcely possible to exaggerate the importance of this last resolution. It marked the solemn union of the two great sections of Irishmen for the purpose of obtaining the recognition of their country's rights. It showed that the old policy of governing Ireland by the division of her sects had failed, and that if the independence of parliament were to be withheld, it must be withheld in opposition to a nation united and in arms" (p. 112).

In March, 1782, Lord North was displaced. Fox became Minister, and the Duke of Portland came over as Lord-Lieutenant.

On March 14th Grattan moved and carried in the Irish House the following emphatic resolution of summons:

"Ordered, That this House be called over on Tuesday, the 16th April next, and that the Speaker do write circular letters to the Members, ordering them to attend that day, as they tender the rights of the Irish Parliament."[1]

Fox now presented to the English House of Commons the following message:

"His Majesty being concerned to find that discontents and

[1] "Grattan's Life and Times," vol. ii. p. 213.

jealousies are prevailing amongst his loyal subjects in Ireland upon matters of great weight and importance, earnestly recommends to this House to take the same into their most serious consideration, in order to such a final adjustment as may give mutual satisfaction to both kingdoms.

"G. R."

Before April 16th, various attempts at delay had been made; but Grattan replied, once for all, that "no answer would be taken as a refusal." Lecky thus describes the scene:

"On April 16, 1782, amid an outburst of almost unparalleled enthusiasm, the declaration of independence was brought forward. A large body of volunteers were drawn up in front of the old Parliament House of Ireland. Far as the eye could stretch the morning sun glanced upon their weapons and on their flags, and it was through their parted ranks that Grattan passed to move the emancipation of his country."

All expected a successful termination to the long struggle, and as soon as the Speaker had taken the chair, the Secretary of State delivered for the Lord-Lieutenant the following message from the English Premier:

"PORTLAND,—

"I have it in command from His Majesty to inform this House that His Majesty being concerned to find that discontents and jealousies are prevailing upon matters of great weight and importance, His Majesty recommends it to this House to take the same into their most serious consideration, in order to such a final adjustment as may give mutual satisfaction to his kingdoms of Great Britain and Ireland."

A message of a similar nature had, on April 9th, been presented to both Houses of the British Parliament.

Mr. Hutchinson, the Secretary of State, said he had no authority to say anything further from the Lord-Lieutenant, but that his appointment was for purposes no doubt beneficial for Ireland; that the great public objects so eagerly sought for were likely to be successful; they could only be obtained by the spirit of the nation, and now that this spirit was universal, it was the duty of the representatives to repeat that public voice and conform to the determined spirit of the nation. He alluded to Mr. Grattan in terms of great respect and admiration, and recommended to the House unanimity and firmness.

Mr. Grattan rose and spoke as follows:

"I am now to address a free people: ages have passed away, and this is the first moment in which you could be distinguished by that appellation. I have only to admire by what heaven-directed steps you have proceeded until the whole faculty of the nation is braced up to the act of her own deliverance.

"I found Ireland on her knees; I watched over her with an eternal solicitude; I have traced her progress from injuries to arms, and from arms to liberty. Spirit of Swift! spirit of Molyneux! your genius has prevailed! Ireland is now a nation! In that new character I hail her! and, bowing to her august presence, I say, '*Esto perpetua!*'

"She is no longer a wretched colony, returning thanks to her governor for his rapine, and to her king for his oppression; nor is she now a squabbling, fretful sectary, perplexing her little wits and firing her furious statutes with bigotry, sophistry, disabilities, and death, to transmit to posterity insignificance and war. . . .

"His Majesty's late ministers imagined they had quelled the country when they had bought the newspapers; they represented us as wild men, and our cause as visionary, and pensioned wretches to abuse both; but we waited and we watched, until the minority became Ireland. Let those ministers now go home and congratulate their king on the redemption of his people. What was the cause? The upper orders, the property, and the abilities of the country, formed with the Volunteer. This united Protestant with Catholic, and the landed proprietor with the people. There was still more than this: there was a continence which confined to limited and legitimate objects; all this kept them innocent, it kept them rational; no vulgar rant against England. They were asserting liberty, according to the frame of the British Constitution, to be enjoyed in perpetual connection with the British Empire. Connected by freedom as well as by allegiance, the two nations, Great Britain and Ireland, form a constitutional confederacy, as well as one empire; the Crown is one link, the Constitution another, and, in my mind, the latter link is the most powerful.

"You can get a king anywhere; but England is the only country with whom you can participate a free Constitution. This makes England your natural connection, and her king your natural, as well as your legal, sovereign, a connection not by conquest, but by compact, and that compact a free Constitution.

"Suffer me now to state some of the things essential to that free Constitution. I will never consent to have men (God knows whom) ecclesiastics, &c., men unknown to the constitution of parliament, and only known to the minister who has breathed into their nostrils an unconstitutional existence, steal to their dark divan to do mischief and make nonsense of bills which their lordships, the House of Lords, or we, the House of Commons, have thought good and fit for the people." [1]

Mr. Grattan then moved, by way of amendment, to lay before His Majesty the causes of Irish discontent, namely, to assure His Majesty that the Commons of Ireland do most sincerely wish that all bills which become law in Ireland should receive the approbation of His Majesty, under the Seal of Great Britain; but that yet we do consider the practice of suppressing our bills in the Council of Ireland, or altering the same anywhere, to be another just cause of discontent. "That an Act 'for the better accommodation of His Majesty's Forces,' being unlimited in duration, is another cause," &c.

These amendments were carried unanimously, and the House adjourned for three weeks, to wait for His Majesty's answer, which arrived on May 27, 1782.

After Grattan's speech of the 16th of April, 1782, the Duke of Portland wrote to Lord Shelbourne on the 26th:

[1] "Grattan's Speeches," edited by his son. Longman, 1822.

"The parliament of Ireland that is to be managed or attended to, it is the whole of this country. It is the Church, the law, the army, the merchant, the tradesman, the manufacturer, the farmer, the labourer, the Catholic, the Dissenter, the Protestant. My opinion is that we should concede to this country the full enjoyment of a free and independent legislature, but that a line should be drawn to prevent their interference in matters of State and external commerce. The consequences of rejecting or delaying would be an end of all government."

On the 28th of April, 1782, Rockingham, with Fox and Shelbourne, being in power, the Duke of Portland wrote to Mr. Fox from Dublin Castle as follows:

"These two points—independence and Mutiny Bill—ceded, and an engagement for settling the judicature and Poyning's law, would incline the Irish to adopt measures and modes of treating, without which I do not see the possibility of settling the business. I foresee very considerable difficulty in drawing the line of that independence which I advised to be conceded, and the embarrassment will increase every day the question is left open. If you delay or refuse to be liberal, government cannot exist here in its present form, and the sooner you recall your Lieutenant, and renounce all claims to this country, the better. But if you concede largely you may make any use of this people and of everything they are worth that you can wish; happy for them that the government shall be in hands that will not take undue advantage of their intoxication."

On the 6th of May, 1782, the Duke wrote to Lord Shelbourne:

"Under the impression of the unavoidable necessity of conceding all the points required, for the sake of deriving any real advantage from the possession of this country, I do recommend that positive assurances be given, that the alteration of the Mutiny Bill, and the modification of Poyning's law, shall be conceded to them in the form required by their address; that the 6th Geo. I. shall be repealed, and that writs of error shall no longer be received by our Court of King's Bench; but that, as Great Britain is desirous not only of satisfying the expectations of the Irish upon all constitutional points, but of preventing every possible source of future jealousy and discontent, . . . also to settle the precise limits of that independence that is required, the consideration that should be given for the protection expected, and the share it would be proper for them to contribute towards the general support of the empire, in pursuance of the declaration contained in the concluding paragraph of their own address. . . . Unless the object is to go fairly to the bottom of the business, and to form a new system of relation between the two countries upon the basis of their mutual interests, the character of the present administration will be lost, and the English Government must be prepared to renounce all pretensions to respect or influence in this country."[1]

On the 6th of June, 1782, there is another letter from the same to the same, touching an Act he hoped shortly to produce securing "the superintending power and supremacy of Great Britain in all matters of State and general commerce;" and on the 22nd of June, about a week before Shelbourne (with Pitt) came into power, another expressing the Duke of Portland's "disappointment and mortification by unexpected changes;" and it appears from a subsequent letter, January 28, 1800, from General Fitzpatrick, who was Secretary at the time to Mr. Grattan, that this very letter of the Duke of Portland's about "imperial and commercial superintendence" was written "within three days of the Duke's instructing the General publicly to disavow any intention of further measures grounded on the second resolution of the British Parliament!" The General then denounces the transaction as "incredibly absurd and puerile," and expresses his "abhorrence of the most shameful and unprincipled violation of a compact, as sacred as history can furnish an example of, between two independent nations." He refers to "what was emphatically styled the final settlement of 1782; and

[1] See "Grattan's Life and Times," by his son.

is ready to bear testimony. He, however, fears "the death-blow to the liberties of Ireland" cannot be averted, and that "the power of corruption will succeed in that measure of outrageous profligacy."[1]

On the 17th of May, the English House went into Committee on the Irish address of April 16th, and Mr. Fox moved a repeal of 6 Geo. I., which was approved by Burke, passed, and received the royal assent on the 21st of June.

On the 27th of May the Irish House met, and the Viceroy, after expressing the utmost satisfaction that immediate attention had been paid, &c., informed them that the British legislature had concurred in a resolution to remove the causes, &c., and "His Majesty commands me to assure you of his disposition to give his assent to Acts to prevent the suppression of bills in the Privy Council of this kingdom, and the alteration of them anywhere; and to limit the duration of the Act for the better regulation of His Majesty's forces in this kingdom to the term of two years."

"On my own part," continued the Duke, "I entertain not the least doubt but that the same spirit which urged you to share the freedom of Great Britain will confirm you in your determination to share her fate also, standing and falling with the British nation."

Mr. Grattan in moving an address in reply said:

"He understood that Great Britain gave up *in toto* every claim to authority over Ireland. He then suggested that £100,000 should be voted, and 20,000 men, to support the British navy; and moved an address, stating that the unqualified repeal of 6 Geo. I. would form a pledge of amity; that they would prepare bills to carry into execution the desires of the people, and that, gratified in these particulars, no constitutional question could exist that would interrupt their harmony."

[1] "Grattan's Life and Times," vol. ii. p. 298.

Independence Recovered. 57

After appointment of a day of public thanksgiving, the following measures were proposed, and passed without opposition.

Grattan brought in a Bill to punish mutiny and desertion, and to repeal the perpetual Mutiny Act. Also to reverse erroneous judgments and decrees (this included writs of error, and settled the final judicature of Ireland).

Mr. Yelverton brought in a Bill to repeal Poyning's law.

Mr. Forbes brought in a Bill for securing the independence of the judges, and the impartial administration of justice, by making their commissions during good behaviour.

Then the delegates from the volunteers of the four provinces of Ireland assembled and declared on the 18th of June, 1782, that they accepted this "complete renunciation."

The Ulster volunteers specially met on the 12th of June and agreed on a similar statement, to be sent to the king; but adding a request for a more equal franchise.[1]

In 1783, the statute 23 Geo. III. c. 28 re-enacted Irish independence. All these measures became the law of the land; and thus was effected without bloodshed a great revolution. The political situation of Ireland underwent a total change, and her liberties and independence appeared finally recovered.

"That was," said Grattan—to whom its success was mainly due, "the age of the repeal of the Penal Code—of the Habeas Corpus Act. The army was made parliamentary; the revenues were made annual, which before had been in greater proportion the perpetual inheritance of the crown; trade became free, it had before by English acts been restrained and annihilated; trade with British colonies became direct; the power of the English Privy Council to originate and alter Irish bills was annihilated;

[1] "Grattan's Life and Times."

the power of the Irish Privy Council to alter, originate, and suppress Irish bills was annihilated; the power of the British Parliament to make laws for Ireland was relinquished; the power of the Irish Parliament, who could before only originate petitions, was restored in full, complete, and exclusive authority."

IRELAND BETRAYED.

"Non regnum, sed magnum latrocinium."—BURKE.

"There is no object which a corrupt minister will not finally ruin—morality, Constitution, commerce, manufactures, agriculture, industry. A corrupt minister issues forth from his cabinet like sin and death, and senates first wither under his footsteps; then he consumes the treasury, and then the capital, the constitutional life, and the moral system; and, at last, the whole island is involved in one capacious curse from shore to shore, from nadir to zenith."—GRATTAN.

"When the warfare of the nations ceased, that of the parliaments began. England then established her supremacy by profligacy on the one side, and prostitution on the other, at the cost of a degraded population, a hireling aristocracy, and a corrupt government."—SYDNEY SMITH.

"The House was composed largely of small boroughs erected purposely to maintain the Protestant ascendency, and which (if concessions were made) could not survive the intended change, hence a revolution in Church and State would follow."—*Private Letter, Portland to Fitzwilliam, February* 16, 1795. S. P. O.

"Every step of conciliating the two descriptions of people that inhabit Ireland, diminishes the probability of a 'union' with England."—WESTMORELAND *to* DUNDAS, *December* 12, 1792.

"The union of a shark with its prey."—LORD BYRON *on Pitt's measure.*

> "As a shark and dogfish wait,
> Under an Atlantic isle,
> For the negro ship whose freight
> Is the theme of their debate,
> Wrinkling their red gills the while."
> PERCY BYSSHE SHELLEY *on Castlereagh and Clare.*

"That Jacobinism which is speculative in its origin may be kept under, but that which arises from penury and irritation, from scorned loyalty and rejected allegiance, has deeper roots. They take their nourishment from the bottom of human nature, and the unalterable constitution of things. Their roots will be shot into the depths of hell, and will at last raise up their proud tops to heaven itself."—BURKE.

"The measures of coercion introduced by the Irish Government, the total rejection of all Mr. Grattan's motions for reform, and, finally, the recall of Lord Fitzwilliam, drove all the more ardent lovers of freedom to despair. 'Non regnum, sed magnum latrocinium,' was the character Burke gave of the Irish Government, and of the system which he said would drive the Irish into Jacobinism. Such, however, was the system which Pitt sanctioned, a system of proscription, corruption, and cruelty."—EARL RUSSELL'S *Life and Times of Charles James Fox*, vol. iii. p. 139.

"There would be no possibility of giving the Irish Church Establishment security in any other way than by a complete incorporation with that of Great Britain. While the present system continued, one minister might wish to uphold the present Establishment, another the system of exclusion, and a third might be desirous to open the Establishment to every claimant. Under such a policy the country would never be quiet. But the Establishment being incorporated, the Protestant would feel himself supported," &c.—CASTLEREAGH *in proposing the Union, February* 5, 1800.

"Before next week it will be impossible for us to take into consideration the different propositions respecting the provisions for Roman Catholic and dissenting clergy, . . . and tithes."—DUKE OF PORTLAND *to* LORD CORNWALLIS, *September* 25, 1800. *Cornwallis Correspondence*, vol. iii. pp. 293, 294.

"Lord Holland says, 'Lord Hobart told me that both he and Lord Clare had been deceived by Mr. Pitt, and that he would have voted against the Union had he suspected any project of extending concessions to Catholics.'"—*Memoirs of the Whig Party*, vol. i. p. 162.

"I believe that half of our majority would be at heart as much delighted as any of our opponents, if the (Union) measure could be defeated."—LORD CORNWALLIS, *Correspondence*, vol. iii. p. 228.

"It was necessary to create some semblance of popular opinion, and Castlereagh began his campaign by drawing £5,000 from the secret service fund, and expended the greater part of it in bribing young lawyers to write pamphlets in favour of a union."—LECKY'S *Grattan*, p. 168.

"Ireland in 1795 was singularly easy to govern, had it been governed honestly, and by honest men."—LECKY.

"It has been said in so many words, it were to be wished the people would rebel. Here is the system, and the principle. From corruption to coercion, and so on to military execution."—BURKE.

IRELAND BETRAYED.

CHAPTER III.

IRELAND BETRAYED.

Pitt, Castlereagh, and "The Union."

"I missed on the scaffold the right honourable gentleman. The treason of the minister was infinitely worse than the rebellion of the people."—GRATTAN.

> "I met murder on the way,
>   He had a masque like Castlereagh,
>   Very smooth he looked, yet grim,
>   Seven bloodhounds followed him."
>   SHELLEY'S *Masque of Anarchy.*

"The Irish Government might have crushed the rebellion, but they let it go on, on purpose to carry the union."—LORD CLONMEL'S *dying statement.*

"His devil went forth. He destroyed liberty and property. He consumed the press; he burned houses and villages; he murdered and he failed."—GRATTAN *on Pitt's terror.*

"Wretches transferred from the table to the dock, and from the dock to the pillory, worked on by fear of death and hope of compensation; who would dip the evangelists in blood, and swear without mercy and without end. You have seen the drunken, worn-out, terrified jury give a verdict of death."—CURRAN.

"The sale of peerages is as notorious as the sale of cast horses in the Castle-yard; the publicity is the same, the terms not very different, the horses not warranted sound, the other animals warranted rotten."—CURRAN.

"A government of panders and runners. Our adjutant sends to the infirmary for the old, and to the brothel for the young—the representatives of the people!"—GRATTAN.

"Well, the minister has destroyed the Constitution. To destroy is easy. The edifices of the mind, like the fabrics of marble, require an age to build: a common labourer and a pickaxe may destroy the one, a little lawyer, a little pimp, and a wicked minister the other."—GRATTAN *on Lord Clare and Pitt.*

THUS Ireland settled the question of independent legislature with a moderation, thoroughness, and nobleness similar, as Hume and Burke opined, to the manner in which England achieved her revolution of 1688.

The independence of 1782 was indeed "a fundamental law," but it was more: it was an international engagement, pledged by the word of the king, by four premiers—Pitt, Shelbourne, Portland, and Fox—and approved by Sheridan, Townshend, Grenville, Grattan, as well as by all, or almost all, the judges. Irish independence was as between nation and nation solemnly, finally, and for ever guaranteed, ascertained, and established. If this was not so, then no nation, no king, no parliament, law, or judge, can ever guarantee anything—force becomes the only remedy, and fraud the only right.

Mr. Fox (debate December 19, 1782, in the English House) declared that his intention "was to give a full, complete, absolute, and perpetual surrender of the British legislature and judicial supremacy over Ireland."

Moreover, as the proceedings adopted by Lord Claremont and Mr. Grattan threw the whole into the form of a treaty, the country got national as well as legal security, and parliament was put in covenant. Fox, as Grattan wrote in 1818, "wished sincerely for the liberty of Ireland without reserve. He was an enemy to an union, and wished the freedom of Ireland to be annexed to his name."

The transaction was, in fact, a treaty between the two countries. First came the resolutions of the Irish House of Commons, and of the volunteers; next a message from the King of England to both houses of the British Parliament; then his message to both houses of the Irish Parliament; fourth, their declaration of rights; fifth, their address to the King, setting forth the rights and claims of Ireland; after which all was submitted to both Houses of Parliament in England; seventh, came the repeal, on the motion of Fox, of the 6 George I. (which had declared the dependency of Ireland); afterwards several Irish Acts repealing Poyning's law, regulating the transmission of bills to Great Britain, and securing the final judicature to Ireland; and ninthly, on the 22nd January, 1783, "the Renunciation Bill," the motion for which, for removing all doubts concerning the exclusive rights of the Parliament and Courts of Ireland, in matters of legislation and judicature, passed without a division. Mr. Townshend moved it, Mr. — afterwards Lord — Grenville seconded, Mr. Fox approved, and Mr. Pitt "was happy to find the House unanimously agreed."

It was a national contract, binding not only parliaments, but countries; it was a solemn treaty, and not only a statute of either country. A statute binds the people, but not the parliament. According to the law of nations, a treaty binds both. As Burke said, "This I call making Ireland free with a vengeance." Fox consulted Mr.—afterwards Lord—Kenyon and Mr. Lee, who were Attorney- and Solicitor-General in England in 1782, when the Bill passed, and their opinion was that the simple repeal had terminated all British jurisdiction over Ireland. Lord Camden said to Grattan, "It is folly talking of simple repeal, the business is done." Thus the Chief Justices of the three courts, the two judges, together with the English authorities, Lords Camden, Kenyon, and Erskine, Mr. Lee, Sir Arthur Piggott, and Sir Samuel Romilly, all agreed in opinion with Mr. Grattan, Lord Charlemont, and Mr. Fox. And when the Duke of Portland prorogued the Irish Parliament on January 27, 1782, he stated in his speech that "to settle the Constitution of Ireland on a secure foundation, and to unite its interests and affections with those of Great Britain, was the principal object of his administration; and he was happy to learn that Parliament considered these objects as accomplished."

At a meeting of the Whig Club in London, May 6, 1800, Fox said:

"It was the most arrogant of all pretensions to pretend that we can legislate for Ireland—that we should understand all her local interests better than herself. The sovereignty of the people—that man shall be his own governor—is the fundamental principle of all well constituted states. To undertake to legislate for persons with whose local interests we must be unacquainted is despotism, not liberty; and the attempt to govern for them was the most audacious which the history of mankind recorded." [1]

The witnesses as to the healing and redeeming effect of the eighteen years of Irish legislation, one and all testify to the same effect. " Her laws," said Lord Plunket, of this 1782-1800 period, " were well arranged and administered—a Constitution fully recognized and established; her revenues, trade, manufactures thriving beyond hope or example of any other country of her extent:" and Lord Clare affirmed that " no country in the world ever made such rapid advance in cultivation and commerce, agriculture and manufactures, with the same rapidity in the same time."

The bankers and merchants of Dublin, the Mayor in the chair, resolved in meeting, December 18, 1798:

"That since the renunciation in 1782 by Great Britain of the right to legislate for Ireland, commerce and prosperity have eminently increased. That we attribute these blessings to the Irish Parliament. That we look with abhorrence on any attempt to deprive the people of Ireland of their parliament. That legislative union would be highly dangerous and impolitic. That the Lord Mayor sign these resolutions, and that the same be published in all the public papers."

And the Right Hon. John Foster, Speaker of the Irish House of Commons, declared, April 11, 1799, that

"The Constitution has showered down upon you more blessings, trade, affluence, than ever fell to your lot in double the time. Will you be cajoled, duped, or threatened into a surrender of it?"

[1] "Grattan's Life and Times," vol. v. p. 197. Colburn, 1846.

In those eighteen years, 1782-1801, the nation sprang into manhood at once, the population 1782-1803 increased, the country had become cultivated. During that period no nation advanced so much in cultivation, commerce, agriculture, and manufactures. Irish exports had increased one-half, and population one-third. Her agriculture fed her people. In 1782 Ireland exported £3,300,000; in 1792 £11,000,000. In 1784 24,000,000 yards of linen; in 1792 45,000,000 yards.

Irish labour was cheap, her water power enormous, and the climate eminently suited the cotton manufactory. English Acts of Parliament destroyed Irish manufactures, especially the woollen, and then crushed out all industrial enterprise, excluded the mass of the people from all other means of existence than agriculture, and produced the land hunger which has caused disturbance and distress.[1]

"Is Ireland," asked Burke in 1778, "united to the Crown of Great Britain for no other purpose than to counteract the bounty of Providence in her favour?"

"Its journals" (Irish Parliamentary), says Lecky, "show a minute attention to industrial questions, to the improvement of means of communication, to the execution of public works. In the last years of the Irish Parliament the material progress was rapid and uninterrupted. In ten years from 1782 the exports more than trebled."

"At present (1785)," said Lord Sheffield, "perhaps the improvement of Ireland is as rapid as any country ever experienced."

In 1818 Messrs. Whitelaw and Walsh, Protestant clergymen, in a history of Dublin, showed the ruin inevitably wrought on Dublin itself by this union :

"When it possessed a parliament it had a press, which the union practically destroyed. Of 66 newspapers, 54 were then

[1] See "Life and Death of the Irish Parliament."

extinct, and the effect on university and city, intellect and life, was as deplorable as the departure of the temporal and spiritual peers, and of the 300 ordinary members."

Colonel Hutchinson, on June 14, 1811, said in the English House that "a free trade, upon no duties, or equal ones, was the principle of the Union. Would they restore to Ireland all she had lost by the degrading and abominable measure of the Union?" Upon this the Speaker remarked: "Such is not the language which it becomes this House to hear of a grave and solemn act of parliament." Colonel Hutchinson then proceeded: "When the Union was first proposed I foresaw in it danger to England, and in the danger, degradation, and ruin of Ireland."

On the commercial as well as political advantages of Irish independence O'Connell is an important—perhaps the most important—witness.[1]

"The admission of the Catholics to the tenancy of lands in 1778 increased considerably the rents of the Protestant landlords in Ireland. The permission to Catholics, in 1782, to purchase estates enhanced enormously the value of the property of all the Protestants of Ireland. Conciliation and prosperity went hand in hand. . . . The Irish Parliament, which asserted the legislative independence of Ireland, was not only the most advantageous to its constituents, but was, at the same time, the most loyal to the British Crown and the most useful to the British power. It was that Parliament which voted and paid the 20,000 Irish Catholics who rushed to man the British fleets, and contributed to Rodney's victory. Ireland never had a parliament more attached to British connection than the Irish Parliament which asserted Irish legislative independence.

"Ten years followed of great and increasing prosperity in Ireland. . . . No country ever rose so rapidly in trade, manufactures, commerce, agricultural wealth, and general prosperity, as Ireland did from the year 1782 until the year 1798, when the 'fomented rebellion' broke out."

[1] Memoir, dedicated to the Queen, pp. 23-26.

But two-thirds of Irish land was held by the grantees of confiscation. Twenty-five landowners commanded the votes of 116 members of parliament. The Irish pension list amounted to £1,020,000 a year. Three families—Devonshire, Ponsonby, Beresford—commanded 60 members of parliament. It was this irresponsible Protestant oligarchy that ruined the nation.

"The English Government," said Burke, in 1796, "has farmed out Ireland to the little narrow faction that domineers there. It is little less than a breach of order even to mention Ireland in the Commons of Great Britain. If the people of Ireland were to be flayed alive by the predominant faction, it would be the most critical of all attempts to discuss the subject."

From 1782 to 1800 the Irish Government consisted practically of the Lord-Lieutenant, who was a creature of the English Prime Minister, and his Secretary—the one generally an English Member of Parliament, the other an English nobleman. There was no Irish Government responsible to the Irish Parliament and nation.

"The country was placed," as Grattan said in 1790, "in a sort of interval between the ceasing of a system of oppression, and the forming of a system of corruption. The latter will take time to propagate all its poisons into the mass of the country; but go on for ten or twelve years," said he, in words that have proved prophetic; "go on as you have the last five; increase in the same proportion your number of parliamentary places; increase, as you have done, your annual charge every five years of peace £183,000; get every five years new taxes, and apply them as you have done, and then the minister will find that he has impaired the trade and agriculture, as well as destroyed the virtue and the freedom of the country."[1]

To understand the triumph of Pitt's Government in this business, it must be borne in mind that Lord North, the worst minister England ever had, and who lost America,

---

[1] "Grattan's Speeches," edited by his son. Longman, 1822.

was in power from 1770 to March, 1782. The Marquis of Rockingham, with Fox and Lord Shelbourne Secretaries of State, and Burke in the administration, was Premier from March to the 1st of July, 1782, the day of his lamented and sudden death. Him the Earl of Shelbourne, with Pitt for Chancellor, succeeded until December; the Coalition Ministry, Portland, North, Fox, and Burke, coming in only until April, 1783, to be followed by Pitt's long administration.

On the 5th of January, 1790, Lord Westmoreland came over to Ireland to govern by corruption. He avowed it, and he practised it, and his appointment, says Alison,[1] was the signal for fierce contests between the Government and the people. The Dissenters of the North coalesced with the Roman Catholics in a loud and menacing demand for reform. Grattan met the situation by a series of tremendous attacks bearing on the menace of Westmoreland's mission, the first of which was delivered on the 1st of February, 1790:

"Above two-thirds of the returns of this House are private property—of those returns many actually this very moment sold to the minister; the number of placemen and pensioners sitting in this House equal near one-half of the whole efficient body. The minister will defeat the attempts of parliament by corruption, and deter the repetition of her attempts by threatening the repetition of the expenses of corruption. Having been long the bawd, corruption will become the sage and honest admonitress of the nation. She will advise her no more to provoke the minister to rob the subject—she will advise her to serve in order to save. Parliament, that giant that purged these islands of the race of tyrants, whose breed it was the fortune of England to preserve, and of Ireland to adopt; parliament, whose head has for ages commerced with the wisdom of the gods, and whose foot has spoken thunder and deposition to the oppressor, will, like the sacred giant, stand a public spectacle shorn of his strength, for the

[1] "Life of Castlereagh," vol. i. pp. 26, 27.

amusement of his enemies, and do feats of ignominious power to gratify an idle and hostile court; and these walls, where once the public weal contended, and the patriot strove, will resemble the ruin of some Italic temple, and abound not with senators, but with animals of prey in the guise of senators, chattering their pert debates, and disgracing those seats that once belonged to the people. You have no adequate responsibility in Ireland, and politicians laugh at the sword of justice, which falls short of their heads, and only precipitates on their reputations."[1]

On the 20th of February, 1790, Grattan moved for a select committee to inquire into the sale of peerages and the purchase of seats.

"Sir," he said, "we persist to combat the project to govern this country by corruption. The sale of honours is an impeachable offence, but they have applied the money arising from such sale to model the House of Commons. This is another impeachable offence. The minister who sells the honour of one House to model the representation of the other, makes them auxiliary, not to support, but to contaminate one another, and corrupt also the dispensation of justice, and the fountains of the law. The ministers of the Crown have introduced a traffic and brokerage of honours. The minister first will buy the question, and then favour you with the forms of debating it. He will cry up parliament when venal, and cry it down when it feels remorse. The minister will soon procure a legislature to adopt any measure according as the divan of the Castle shall give its janissaries here the word of command. Ireland was sold for £1,500,000 formerly, and, if opposition persists, will be sold again."

"Sir," said Grattan, on the 26th of the same month—"I said that His Majesty's ministers had sold the peerages, for which offence they were impeachable. I said they had applied the money for the purpose of purchasing seats in the Commons for the servants and followers of the Castle, and were impeachable as public malefactors, and I dared them to inquiry. I repeat those charges now; and if anything more severe was expressed,

[1] See "Life and Times," vol. iii. pp. 445-8.

I will again repeat it. Why not expel me now? Why not send me to the bar of the House of Lords? Going out of this house I shall repeat my sentiments, that His Majesty's ministers are guilty of impeachable offences; and advancing to the bar of the Lords, I shall repeat those sentiments; or if the Tower be my habitation, I will there meditate impeachment, and return not to capitulate, but to punish."[1]

"The Irish Government," said Grattan, in 1791, "is a cypher. The control exclusively placed in the Lord-Lieutenant's Secretary on that bench, makes him more forcible than Demosthenes, more persuasive than Tully—like Solomon in all his glory, sitting among his State concubines.

"The people of Ireland would not consent to be governed by the British Parliament; an expedient was devised—let the Irish Parliament govern the people of Ireland, and Great Britain govern the Irish Parliament.

"The path of treachery in a principal country leads to the block, but in a nation governed like a province, to the helm.

"By this trade of parliament the king is absolute. Both houses are as much an instrument in his hand as a bayonet in the hands of a regiment. Like a regiment, we have our adjutant, who sends to the infirmary for the old, and to the brothel for the young, and men carted thus into the house are representatives of the people! Suppose General Washington to ring his bell, and order his servants out of livery to take their seats in Congress. The trade in parliament is like original sin, it operates through all political creation.

"Of three hundred members above two hundred are returned by individuals, forty to fifty by ten persons: several boroughs have no resident elector; some but one. The great majority are chosen by individuals, and a great proportion afterwards endowed by the Crown."[2]

On January 19, 1792, the session began which, at Pitt's bidding, was to open the sluices, and make rebellion inevitable. So far (April) the Catholic committees had

[1] "Grattan's Life and Times," vol. iii. p. 457.
[2] See "Grattan's Speeches"—Reform in Parliament, 1793.

trusted to expectations held out by England. Their petition had been flung back in their faces. Pitt, if still in their favour, was unable or unwilling to force his wishes on the Parliament. Neither the Chancellor nor Lord Westmoreland had any doubt of their power to check this new movement on one condition, that they could be sure of being backed by the Cabinet. There needed still (October) but a firm word from England for faction to slink into its den, and that word was not spoken; but on January 23, 1793, Dundas wrote to Westmoreland that the Catholics were less likely to concur in disturbing the existing order of things when they participate in the franchise.

Pitt was vexed and offended with Ireland on account of her conduct in 1785 on the commercial proposition, and in 1789 on the Regency, when the Irish Parliament wished to concentrate the right regal power in the hands of the Regent, instead of putting so much in those of Pitt. He thought one parliament would be more handy than two, and his direct object (as shown in his letter to the Duke of Rutland, October 7, 1784), was "to unite the Protestant interest in excluding the Catholics from any share in the representation or government of the country." Pitt managed the king by threatening to "let loose Fox upon him," and thus made the king too strong. As soon as the king, in 1801, found this out, he turned Pitt out, and Pitt only regained power by a private pledge to the king, in 1804, against the Catholics.

"The aspect of affairs in 1793," says Alison, "became so threatening that Earl Fitzwilliam was sent over in December, 1794, to succeed Lord Westmoreland, and he came over avowedly as the organ of a conciliatory policy, his mission . . . to concede Catholic emancipation, and such a measure of parliamentary reform as might be consistent with the preservation of order, and of the monarchical constitution in Church and State. These favourable dispositions were increased by the offer to Grattan of an important place in the administration, on whose motion the House of Commons voted £3,000,000 to the English Government to carry on the war—a very large sum for a country whose revenue was only £1,800,000."

English Protestants, however, took alarm at Grattan's proposed concessions to Roman Catholics; and the English Government disavowed those proposals, and after the three million vote had passed both Irish Houses, recalled Fitzwilliam, and the whole liberal Irish administration went out of office. Lord Camden succeeded Lord Fitzwilliam. Lord Westmoreland wrote to Dundas, December 12, 1792, that "Every step of conciliating the two descriptions of people that inhabit Ireland, diminishes the probability of that object to be wished—a union with England;" and Mr. Froude writes on that as follows:

"The language in which Westmoreland speaks of the union seems to show that it was already the object at which the Cabinet was aiming. If the object most to be feared was the drawing together of Catholics and Protestants, the readiest way for England to prevent it was to force emancipation upon the present parliament, and to make the Catholics feel that they owed their relief to the English ministers. The union might then be accomplished in time to prevent serious mischief. This interpretation renders conduct explicable which otherwise might have appeared delirious."[1]

The Catholic question was the supreme one. The Catholics had enjoyed the suffrage till 1727, and Grattan insisted that "the removal of their disabilities is necessary to make the Catholic a freeman, and the Protestant a people." On February 20, 1792, he said:

"I now press upon you the final and external doom to which some propose to condemn the Catholic. What! never be free? Three million of your people condemned to everlasting slavery! Never to be free! do you mean to tell the Roman Catholic, in

[1] "The English in Ireland," book viii. p. 79.

vain you take oaths of allegiance, it will make no difference as to your emancipation. Go to France, go to America, carry your property, industry, manufactures, and family to a land of liberty. This is a sentence which requires the power of a God, the malignity of a demon."

Grattan, however, was defeated by 208 against 25; and later, when Pitt had deliberately availed himself of the popularity of supposed concessions and of Lord Fitzwilliam, and the Irish Parliament had voted heavy burdens and great military establishments, then Pitt abandoned his principles, deceived, used, and recalled Lord Fitzwilliam, and prepared for the insurrection and the Union.

Pitt's Act of 1793 gave Catholic freeholders the franchise, but Government feared that the union of Catholics, Presbyterians, Dissenters, and Republicans would change the Constitution from a mixed monarchy into a republic, or a monarchy in which the real power was vested in the people who might tamper with the Church.[1] *The real crux was Grattan's motion that Catholics sit in parliament.* Earl Camden, the new Lord-Lieutenant, took the final stand (1793), that Catholics should not sit, and thus he wrote privately to Lord Castlereagh,[2] who was appointed Chief Secretary April 17, 1799, having performed the duties, however, for two years previously.

"On February 4, 1793, Major Hobart proposed to admit Catholics to the franchise, magistracy, and grand juries. The day after, a Bill was introduced forbidding the possession of guns or powder without license. This Act was sentence of death to the volunteer corps. On February 6th, a militia was moved for, which would produce 16,000 men, and at the same time a proposal made to increase the regular army to 20,000 men."[3]

---

[1] Alison's "Life of Castlereagh," vol. i. p. 19.
[2] February 4, 1793, MS. "Londonderry Papers" and "Castlereagh Correspondence," vol. i. p. 12.
[3] Froude, "The English in Ireland," book viii. p. 90.

"So armed, Hobart was able to insist. The second reading passed with only three dissentients, but the proposal in committee to admit Catholics to parliament was defeated 163 to 69. Those in the House who would have given the Catholics nothing were by far the largest number. Had the Castle offered a full measure of emancipation, the profligate Whig aristocracy would have rallied the country on the Protestant cry against perfidious England. Had the Catholic petition been rejected in London, they were ready to open their arms to their oppressed fellow-citizens, . . . and so reign themselves."

On July 8, 1793, Fitzgibbon introduced the Convention Bill into the Lords, declaring the assemblage of bodies of men calling themselves representatives, under any pretence, illegal.

"The landlords had sown the wind, and were to reap the whirlwind. The Irish nation, as it is passionate and revengeful, so beyond most others it is malleable by just authority. The Celtic earth-tiller will repay his liege lord for kindness and generosity with romantic fidelity. Two centuries had been allowed the Saxon intruder to win the affections of the native race. The Irish peasants remained in rags like their ancestors; lodged under one roof with their pigs and cows; paying rent to masters who had no care for their bodies; paying tithes to clergy who cared as little for their souls; maintaining gallantly in the midst of their wretchedness their own hedge schools and priests. So it had gone on till they were told their chain was broken, . . . and that if they wanted more than the privilege of sending one of their Protestant masters to parliament, they must arm."[1]

On a few pages further on (p. 113) Mr. Froude's sympathies have veered right round, for he proceeds:

"The Irish peasant, if let loose and told to be his own governor, flies at the hand which has unlocked his chains. Pitt had taken a step which made the union a certainty, but no less certainly a desperate and bloody insurrection. . . .

[1] Froude, "The English in Ireland," book viii. pp. 107, 108.

"In 1794 the Cabinet was modified by the accession of the moderate Whigs, and in August Grattan and others were invited to London, and saw Pitt, who let Grattan go away with the impression that although the admission of Catholics to parliament would not be made a Government measure, it would not be opposed. Pitt was thinking of an union, but his ignorance of the country must have been extraordinary, even in an English Prime Minister, if he could dream that Catholic Ireland, in constitutional possession of the power which the majority would confer, would then be persuaded to part with her ascendency."[1]

In August, 1794, Lord Fitzwilliam, on his coming appointment to succeed the Duke of Portland, wrote to Grattan for his assistance, saying, " Except during the administration of the Duke, I believe you never have approached the Castle in confidence." Grattan remarked that " Ireland was not handy enough for Pitt; " he could not easily manage her.

In October, 1794, Pitt made overtures to Grattan; but the latter's old friend, Denis Daly, Muster-Master-General, who had been in office under Pitt, said he " was a bad minister for Ireland." Gerald Hamilton said, " I would not trust Pitt; he'll cheat you." Mr. Sergeant Adair said, " If you have any dealings with Pitt he'll cheat you; I never would act with him except I had pen, ink, and paper." Grattan told Pitt the essential question was the Catholic. Pitt replied, " If Government were pressed to yield it." " Such," Grattan said, " were the identical expressions." Grattan declined office. Lord Fitzwilliam was satisfied he had full powers on that question, and said so to Burke. Pitt threw obstacles in the way of arrangements with Lord Fitzwilliam; and the Duke of Portland told Grattan that the jobs or appointments made by Pitt were " scandalous." Lord Fitzwilliam, however, was appointed, and arrived in Dublin.[2] His answers to ad-

---

[1] Froude, " The English in Ireland," book viii. p. 123.
[2] " Grattan's Life and Times," vol. iv. pp. 178-182.

dresses seemed to promise a period of conciliation and progress in strict accordance with arrangements made in London by Pitt, Portland, Fitzwilliam, and Grattan. Measures accordingly were eagerly looked for by the people, when Lord Fitzwilliam's recall began to be rumoured.

Parliament opened on January 22, 1795; and on February 14th even Fitzgibbon wrote Pitt that nothing but the Catholic Relief Bill could save the country. The real difficulty was explained in the private letter from the Duke of Portland to Lord Fitzwilliam, February 16th (State Paper Office), that [to yield must change the constitution of the House of Commons, which would then overthrow the Church Establishment. The *House was composed largely of members for small boroughs erected purposely to maintain the Protestant ascendency*, and which could not survive the intended change, hence a revolution in Church and State would follow.

On Lord Fitzwilliam's departure the people drew his carriage to the water-side, shops were closed, the houses hung in mourning. Grattan's Bill was out-voted; insurrection came on; Protestant ascendency organized; and in 1798 the Orange organization had broken the right arm of insurrection.

September 3, 1794, Burke wrote to Grattan from Beaconsfield respecting Robert Burke, his son, lately deceased:

"His eye was fixed on Ireland to the last hour of his life, and his eye was fixed on you as the only man who could serve it essentially—as the only man who could save it. He never spoke to any one on the subject without expressing this sentiment; nor have I ever spoken, nor shall I ever speak any language than his, because it was always the language of truth and wisdom. You have given to Ireland the great, but critical and perilous, blessings of liberty and independence."

In 1795 Burke also wrote of the hopes of the new Irish session, and of his confidence in Lord Fitzwilliam's noble views, and in Grattan's opposition leadership; and he distinguishes between the constitutional and political independence of Ireland.

"I could not pray to God for a greater security to you for everything you hold dear; for in that time Lord Fitzwilliam's virtues (the greatest and most unmixed that I have known in man) would bring the leading men of the nation into habits of moderation, lenity, equity, and justice, which the practice of some hundreds of years, and the narrow hard-heartedness of a monarchy, have banished from the minds of many of them. Ireland constitutionally is independent, politically she never can be so. It is a struggle against nature. She must be protected. France has not the means of either serving or hurting her that are in the hands of Great Britain.

"If Grattan, by whom I wish the Catholics to be wholly advised, thinks differently from me, I wish the whole unsaid. You see Lord Fitzwilliam sticks nobly to his text, and neither abandons his cause nor his friends, though he has few indeed to support him. Surely Great Britain and Ireland ought to join in wreathing a never-fading garland for the head of Grattan."

And March 3rd Burke wrote to Grattan himself:

"I feel as much joy as my poor broken heart is capable of receiving from the manner in which the Irish session has opened. Ireland resolved to live and die with Great Britain. More troops were raised and greater sums voted than before was ever known. I really thought everything was settled. Please God, whilst one link hangs to another I will not be untrue to you. The monarchy is as much obliged to you, at least, as any subject the king has."

Yet Lord Fitzwilliam stated in the English Lords, "For having connected myself with Mr. Grattan, I am dismissed; for it was obviously on that account, chiefly, that I incurred the hostility of the English minister;" and April 21, 1795, Grattan declared in the House that

"Catholic emancipation was not only the concession of the British Cabinet, but its precise engagement." He moved then for a committee on the state of the nation. Pitt's perfidy was about to be proved by the man who had treated with Pitt, and whose word and whose principles were sacred, and a division of 158 to 48 against the exposure was Pitt's only possible answer.

At this time, 1795, the debt of the Irish nation was £3,820,000; five years later, at the union, £25,000,000; a few years after, £150,000,000; and in 1816 Ireland was proclaimed bankrupt.

Mr. Pitt's Government had passed a Convention Act, a Riot Act, an Arms Act, a Gunpowder Act, an Insurrection Act, an Indemnity Act, and a suspension of the Habeas Corpus Act; they imprisoned without bail and transported without trial; spies and informers swarmed, the prisons overflowed, riot defied "the terror," a military despotism was established, and Grattan, in the Irish House, could only muster 16 against 127; Fox could only muster 84 against 220.

"'The Government,' said Grattan, "renounce economy, trample on rights, laugh at opinion, sell the peerage, model the representation, and not only practise, but avow the arts of corruption. If the most ambitious aristocracy were to become the Ministry, they would possess at least one advantage, they would be a Government of gentlemen."

Listen now to the great advocate, Curran, as in 1797 and 1798 he describes some of the meaner of Pitt's instruments:

"Let me ask you honestly, what do you feel when called on to give a verdict which every man of you knows to be utterly and absolutely false? I speak not of those wretches so often transferred from the table to the dock, and from the dock to the pillory. I speak of the miscreants who avowed upon their oaths that they had come from the very seat of government—the Castle—worked upon by the fear of death and the hope of compensation to give evidence; from these catacombs of living death, where the wretch is buried a man and is then dug up a witness. I have heard of assassination by sword, pistol, and dagger; but here is a wretch who would dip the evangelists in blood, ready to swear without mercy and without end. If he will swear, let it be on the knife, the proper symbol of his profession. . . .

"You have seen the drunken, worn-out, and terrified jury give a verdict of death, and when returning sobriety brought back their consciences, prostrate themselves before the humanity of the Bench, that mercy might save their consciences from eternal self-condemnation, and their souls from innocent blood."[1]

In 1797, a secret committee of the English House of Commons reported disunion, and England, that is, the English minister and the Castle junto, had resolved on the downward course.

And now, in 1796, came the closing words, as of *judgment and doom*, from the mighty master, Burke. They tell us—what now we have learnt and know from events—of the necessary results of England's folly, and they came almost from Burke's own death-bed, as certainly from the death-bed of Irish loyalty:

"That Jacobinism . . . which arises from penury and irritation, from scorned loyalty and rejected allegiance, has deeper roots. They take their nourishment from the bottom of human nature, and the unalterable constitution of things. Their roots will be shot into the depths of hell, and will at last raise up their proud tops to heaven itself."

"In what all this will end," added Burke, "it is not impossible to conjecture, though the exact time cannot be fixed as you would calculate an eclipse. Lord Fitzwilliam could not live long in power because he was a true patriot."

In 1797, to assist the union, parliamentary reform had been rejected in order to bring the Irish Parliament

[1] "Grattan's Life and Times."

into contempt, and parliamentary corruption had the like effect. Grattan demanded the right to elect representatives and freedom of religion—" Reform parliament, and let the king identify himself with his people. Try this plan, as the ultimate consequence of a union will be separation."

Pitt was becoming unpopular in England. It was the same Pitt who said, " Take the children for the factories, that the men may go to the wars." The seamen at the Nore mutinied; his arms and negotiations failed; even his attempt to hang his early friends, Horne Tooke, Hardy, and others, failed; and upwards of thirty counties and cities in England passed addresses praying the king to remove Pitt from the royal councils for ever. Irish addresses concluded with the same prayer, after arraigning Pitt's policy " before their country, the whole British Empire, before the king, in the face of the world, in the presence of God." Similar resolutions passed unanimously at a meeting of the bar, all present (74) signing; but Pitt's answer was to suppress by the soldiery all meetings.

In " A Letter to my Fellow Citizens," Grattan concluded his exposure of Pitt's iniquities thus :

"The half million, said the minister, that is my principle of attraction. Among the rich I send my half million, and I despatch my coercion among the people. His devil went forth—he destroyed liberty and property, he consumed the Press, he burned houses and villages, he murdered, and he failed."

The same sentiments we find re-echoed by Lord Byron, on the 21st of April, 1812, in one of the three speeches which were all he ever delivered in the English House of Lords :

"That union, so called, as *lucus a non lucendo*, a union from never uniting, which in its first operation gave a death-blow to the independence of Ireland, and in its last may be the cause of her eternal separation from this country. If it must be called a union, it is the union of the shark with his prey; the spoiler swallows up his victim, and they become one and inseparable. Thus has Christ Britain swallowed up the parliament, the constitution, the independence of Ireland."

On the 15th of January, 1797, Sir Lawrence Parsons, afterwards Lord Rosse, moved an amendment against "Union." He argued that:

"The minister had recommended an incorporating union with England. He had prevented the House from giving an answer to His Majesty in the preceding session by a sudden prorogation, and he now wished to prevent their giving an answer at all. He had employed the most unwarrantable means to pervert the sentiments of parliament on the subject, appointing places to corrupt and pack the House of Commons, while the country was covered with armies greater than were ever known before, while martial law prevailed, and English ministers hoped to destroy the independence of Ireland. The internal legislation of Ireland had been secured by the original contract of Henry II., and by the Great Charter of King John; it had been ratified by Henry III., consecrated by a usage of six hundred years, and confirmed by the final settlement of 1782: absentees would be increased by a union, and Great Britain lose her best security. The country was too great for an external parliament. He moved the following amendment:

"'Humbly to assure His Majesty that this kingdom is inseparably united with Great Britain, and that it is the sentiment, wish, and real interest of all, that it shall ever so continue in the full enjoyment of the blessings of a free constitution, in the support of the honour and dignity of His Majesty's crown, and in the preservation and advancement of the welfare and prosperity of the whole empire,'" &c.

The supporters of this amendment contended that the settlement of 1782, instead of tending to separation, cemented the connection between the two countries. That in 1782, when more than 80,000 volunteers were in arms, when invasion was threatened, and when England had lost her American empire, Ireland did not think of separation, she stood firm by England, she stood by her parliament; by that body obtained the Octennial Bill, the Mutiny Bill, the repeal of Poyning's law, the independence of her judges, the restoration of her appellant jurisdiction, her free trade, and, finally, her free constitution; that the local and internal improvements of the country were owing to her resident parliament and resident gentry. They further stated that, while the Habeas Corpus Act was still suspended, and martial law was still in existence, and an overwhelming military force in the country, such a measure should not be brought forward.

On January 22, 1797, in the Irish House, Mr. G. Ponsonby moved the following amendment to the address:

"That it is the undoubted birthright of the people of Ireland to have a free and independent legislature resident within the kingdom, such as was asserted by the parliament of the kingdoms in 1782, and acknowledged and ratified by His Majesty and the Parliament of Great Britain upon the final adjustment of the differences between the two countries."

But why, it may be asked, after independence was granted, did Irish disorders increase?

On March 23, 1797, came Fox's summary in the English House of the causes of Irish discontent. Let him answer the question. The terms of his motion on the state of Ireland were, "that an humble address, &c., and to adopt such healing and lenient measures, &c., and to conciliate the affections of all descriptions of His Majesty's subjects." He argued that it must appear to many very extraordinary that since 1782 discontent has gone on increasing. It was clear that the people had not that influence in the House of Commons which should exist in a free constitution. The defect arose from the vicious state of the representation. Five-sixths of the inhabitants were Roman

Catholics, and excluded. An opinion prevailed that the influence of the Executive counteracted the benefits which the legislative branch of the Constitution had obtained. In 1789 the Lord-Lieutenant and the Irish Parliament had differed, and the Lord-Lieutenant was censured by the Irish Parliament, upon which the influence of the Executive was in a most unconstitutional manner openly and corruptly exerted, and Parliament unsaid all it had said before. It was matter of notoriety that a regular system was then devised for enslaving Ireland.

"To appease and allay the great discontent, I proposed the complete independence of Ireland. The principle was, above all, ... to restore that cordial affection between the two countries so eminently requisite to the preservation and prosperity of both.",

Fox then goes on:

"A systematic plan of corruption. The measure of 1782 had been rendered completely inefficacious. Ireland was placed in a state of degradation beyond any former period. Persevering and avowed system of duplicity. My abhorrence of such a truly diabolical maxim. Mankind are not to be treated in this manner. If you do not allay their discontent, there is no way but force,—to risk a civil war. I would have the whole Irish government regulated by Irish notions and prejudices. The more Ireland is under the Irish Government, the more will she be bound to British interests."[1]

"A person of high consideration (Lord Chancellor Clare) was known to say that half a million had been spent in quelling opposition, and that half a million more should be expended. Peerages had been sold; proof offered; Parliament refused to listen. The independence of the Irish Parliament was but a name. 'The Executive was everything; the people nothing.'"

In 1794, he continued, Earl Fitzwilliam was sent over

[1] Fox's motion on the state of Ireland, 1797. Hansard, vol. xxxiii. pp. 140–55.

as Lord-Lieutenant, the most popular ever sent. After known preparations for complete emancipation of Roman Catholics, he was of a sudden dismissed, and the entire system changed!

Then commenced a course of violent measures against the people, and inordinate powers were used, until every principle of law and the constitution was effaced, and military force became the desperate resort.

Pitt pretended that to pass this motion would be to menace the independence of the Irish Parliament already destroyed by his policy.

Dr. Duigenan, one of his creatures, moved on May 3, 1797, that Fox's speech was a false, scandalous, and malicious libel on the Irish Parliament.

On May 3, 1797, Grattan delivered his famous defence of independence, and eulogy of Fox's speech of March 23, 1797.

"What an idea has Mr. Fox disclosed as just and applicable to Ireland? an Irish Legislature and an Irish Government, a genuine Executive and a genuine Parliament. *Major rerum nascitur ordo.* No clerk government, no trade in boroughs, no trade of parliament, no trade of blood, no half million, no sale of peerages, no Insurrection Bill, no military executions, no civil wars. As an Englishman he would strengthen the connection by removing the motives of separation. This is an idea worthy a comprehensive statesman. He applies to great passions and great principles for the government of a great country. Measure his abilities by the gigantic proportions of the calamities he would have prevented—by the American Empire which his advice would have preserved; by the 250 millions sterling debt for two wars his advice would have saved. He stood against the current of the Court; he stood against the tide of the people; he stood against both united. He was the isthmus lashed by the waves of democracy, and by the torrent of despotism, unaffected by either, and superior to both; the Marpesian rock that struck its base to the centre, and raised its forehead to the skies!"[1]

[1] "Grattan's Speeches," vol. iii. pp. 329, &c. Longman, 1822.

"Certain Ruin Coming on."

Throughout this period the Castlereagh correspondence was secretly expressing Castlereagh's absolute conviction that nothing could carry the union but a determination to carry it at all hazard, and by every means.

On the 7th of April, 1797, Fox wrote to Grattan, that in his speech on the affairs of Ireland he had proceeded principally upon the facts and arguments with which Grattan furnished him—that the likeliest " chance of salvation would be a general expression of a wish for Pitt's removal. Ruin almost certain is coming on. I really think the existence of the funded property of England, and the connection between our two countries, depend upon the measures to be taken in a few, a very few, months."

As Grattan said five months later, " Pitt is more likely to depose the king of England than restore the king of France."

Lord Moira, in his motion, November, 1797, declared that men were—

"Tortured on suspicion, picqueted once till they fainted, twice till they fainted, a third time till they fainted. That they were hung up till half hanged to make them confess. Thirty houses had been burnt of a night, because the suspected arms were not brought forth. If the system was not changed he believed Ireland would not remain connected with this country five years longer."

Sheridan's description of the march of Hastings best describes that of the commander in Ireland : " Terror was in his front, rebellion in his rear ; for wherever the heel of oppression was raised, trodden misery sprang up and looked around for vengeance."

In March, 1797, Burke thus wrote :

" My poor opinion is that the closest connection between Great Britain and Ireland is essential to the well-being—I had almost said to the very being—of the two kingdoms. For that purpose the whole of the superior, and what I should call imperial politics, ought to have its residence here; and that Ireland, locally, civilly, and commercially independent, ought politically to look up to Great Britain in all matters of peace and war, and, in a word, with her to live and die. At bottom Ireland has no other choice—I mean rational choice.

"I think, indeed, that Great Britain would be ruined by the separation of Ireland, but it would fall the most heavily on Ireland. By such a separation Ireland would be the most completely undone country in the world."

On the 5th of June, 1797, Burke wrote his last letter:

"I have done with this topic, and perhaps for ever; but I do not wish it concealed that I am of the same opinion to my last breath. The government of Ireland becomes every day more difficult, and the incapacity of the jobbers more and more evident; but as long as they can draw upon England for men and money, they will go on in their jobbing system. Things must take their course."

Burke died 9th of July, 1797, aged 67 years. Irish independence ceased some three years later. Things did take their course, and Grattan also thought he had done with it for ever; and three weeks before Burke's last word on Ireland, we find Grattan retiring in despair from the representation of Dublin and the Irish House of Commons, and thus explaining his withdrawal:

"What is the Irish rebellion? Unanimity against despotism. Two remedies occurred—coercion and conciliation. We opposed the former, we proposed the latter. The Ministry proposed to make the people quiet by a system of laws and proclamations which, had they been quiet before, would have rendered them distracted. The power of limited monarchy was not to be preserved by constitutional action, its natural ally; but by despotic power, its natural death and dissolution. The cause of the Irish disturbance of 1797 was the endeavour to establish by unlimited bribery absolute power. The system of coercion was a necessary consequence and part of the system of corruption; and the two systems would have established a tyranny tremendous and intolerable, imposed on the Senate by influence and the people by arms.

"We have offered you our measure, you will reject it; we deprecate yours, you will persevere. Having no hopes to persuade or dissuade, and having discharged our duty, we shall trouble you no more, and after this day shall not attend the House of Commons."

The leaders of the opposition then seceded. Parliament was prorogued, and then dissolved.

Insurrection broke out. Addresses against the Union were voted from all parts, meanwhile every engine was set to work—there were threats and promises; sheriffs refused to call public meetings; the military interfered with meetings; the Habeas Corpus Act was suspended, and martial law proclaimed; a Rebellion Act had been passed in the preceding session for summary arrest and trial, and all these measures broke the spirit of the nation.

In 1798 the order of the day was to get one man to swear against another, and lodge him in gaol. "Will no one swear against Grattan!" was the cry, and efforts were made by his friends to get him out of the country. When he was in England, according to a memorandum left by his wife, she was privately advised that "if he returned he would certainly be put to death."

The position was thus boldly analyzed and explained in the English House by Sheridan in June of this year:

"When conciliation was held out to the people of Ireland, was there any discontent? When the Government of Ireland was agreeable to the people, was there any discontent? After the prospect of that conciliation was taken away, after Lord Fitzwilliam was recalled, after the hopes which had been raised were blasted, *when the spirit of the people was beaten down*, insulted, despised, I will ask any gentleman to point out a single act of conciliation which has emanated from the Government of Ireland."

"It is the fashion to say, and the address holds the same language, that the rebellion which now rages in the sister kingdom has been owing to the machinations of 'wicked men.' It is indeed to the measures of wicked men that the deplorable state of Ireland is to be imputed. It is to those wicked ministers who have broken the promises they held out, who betrayed the party they seduced into their views to be the instruments of the foulest treachery ever practised against any people. It is to those wicked ministers, who have given up that devoted country to plunder, resigned it a prey to their faction by which it has so long been trampled on, that we owe the miseries into which Ireland has been plunged, and the dangers by which England is threatened."

Thus the murder of a nation was once more resolved on. Ireland had asserted her liberty. "Unanimity had shut the gates of strife, providence had opened those of commerce," and the use of articles of luxury and comfort by the people had increased enormously. *Irish independence had, in fact, succeeded too much.* Mis-representation was in danger; the minority Church was in danger; the monopoly of English merchants was in danger; everything weak, wicked, treacherous, and unjust was in danger from a strong self-governed nation; and so, in 1800, by force, fraud, and bribery, the Irish Parliament ended, and the life and light of Ireland, and the peace of England with it. Ireland was once more to be put into the vivisector's trough. It was this time to be a scientific destruction. The meanness and malignity of the British Government triumphed, persecutors of the people were put in power, and Catholics and Protestants were set by the ears once more; incessant Coercion Acts have signalized the "Union," and the public life of both nations has ever since been degraded and poisoned.

The union was conceived in murder, perjury, and treachery, born in corruption, and baptized in blood. Placemen, pensioners, or officers on the staff, packed all seats Government could command. The bribes were enormous, and military terrorism was rife, yet Government could only get 5,000 to sign petitions for the union against 707,000 the other way.

The stand made by the opposition raised the price of hirelings in the market. One of them, M'Donald, demanded 5,000 guineas, and got them. Charles Bushe and others were assailed with offers so splendid that they staggered them. Grattan used to say "there were only seven men on one side of Government who were not bribed." On the trial of Kirwan, it appeared that the list of the jury came from the pocket of the Under Secretary at the Castle, Sir Charles Saxton.[1] The plan was to spend a million and a half in the purchase of boroughs, £15,000 being awarded for each, and commissioners appointed.

On the 25th of March, 1798, the funded debt amounted to £9,275,000; the next year to £14,920,000; and on 1st of January, 1801, to £26,841,000; in January, 1804, £43,000,000, and £52,500,000 the same year. On the other hand, under the rule of the Irish Parliament, the debt of the nation had diminished from £2,477,000 in 1789, to £2,219,000 in 1793.

In 1798, October 17th, Lord Cornwallis remonstrated with Pitt against "the desperate measure of waging eternal war against Papists and Presbyterians, about nine-tenths of the community."[2] Pitt intended to grant emancipation after the union, but knew that even corrupt Protestant members of parliament might not vote for the union with emancipation included. At this time, October 16, 1798,[3] Lord Clare wrote that "he had seen Mr. Pitt, Lord Eldon, and the Duke of Portland about this damnable country," that emancipation would be left out of the Act of Union, and that Pitt was "fully sensible of the neces-

---

[1] "Grattan's Life and Times," vol. v. p. 118.
[2] See "Cornwallis Correspondence," vol. ii. pp. 418, 419.
[3] "Castlereagh Correspondence," vol. i. pp. 393, 394.

sity of effectual civil control over the Popish clergy, . . . best effected by moderate stipends and Crown licenses for ecclesiastical functions on pain of perpetual banishment."

The opposition was so threatening that Castlereagh went to London (December, 1798) to personally explain. Great efforts were made to extend the time of service of the militia, and Lord Cornwallis wrote the Duke of Portland (December 1, 1798),[1] that if the militia were withdrawn, the union must be abandoned. The English militia regiments in Ireland were thoroughly disgusted with their duty there, and insisted on returning home.

Castlereagh wrote the Government, November 12, 1798, that "if the Catholic and Republican party can convince the Protestant landholders that it is for their interest to join in effecting a separation, the thing is done. Great Britain, with all her naval superiority, could not keep this country. We must not sit with our arms across, and muse and talk as the Scotch did. The matter must be finished in a session."[2]

"The most formidable opposition was among the barristers and citizens of Dublin, the country gentlemen all over Ireland, and the lower ranks of the Orangemen and Protestants of the North. With most of them it was not mere resistance, but absolute horror."[3]

Castlereagh, who managed every detail, sent home a tariff of seats at £1,455,000.

"Opposition became more formidable as the time approached, especially in the North, the stronghold hitherto of Protestantism and attachment to the British connection.

"Cornwallis and Castlereagh in vain exerted themselves to the utmost to win over or neutralize the Protestant magnates, hitherto the chief supporters of Government. Pitt exerted him-

---

[1] "Cornwallis Correspondence," vol. ii. p. 454.
[2] "Memoir on Union," Correspondence, vol. i. pp. 442, 443.
[3] Alison's "Life of Castlereagh. "See also " Castlereagh Correspondence," vol. ii. p. 51.

self personally to win over or neutralize the most important opponents, but with very little effect. . . .

"Martial law was proclaimed in Antrim and Mayo, and on the 23rd of January, 1799, a majority of one—106 to 105—passed the address, reversed two nights after, on Sir L. Parson's motion, by a majority of five. Dublin was thrice illuminated, and the blaze of bonfires was seen far and wide on the mountains. Delay was then resorted to, and a tour to the North was arranged by the Lord-Lieutenant and the Court, who held private *interesting* conferences with leading opponents."[1]

"Nothing short of the entire destruction of their opponents would satisfy either of the parties. The whole of the South is prepared to rise the moment a French soldier sets his foot on shore. The union agitation had alienated the Orangemen and Protestants."[2]

The merchant Guild of Dublin, an ultra-Protestant incorporation, issued an address calling on all classes and sects to unite against the union, and returning their warmest thanks to their Roman Catholic fellow-citizens in Dublin for their manly and patriotic conduct.

Lord Cornwallis wrote (February 4, 1800): "The capital quite in an uproar. Some of our unwilling supporters in Parliament decline giving further support. God only knows how the business will terminate; but it is so hard to struggle against the private interests, and the pride and prejudices of a nation, that I shall never feel confident of success till the union is actually carried."[3] And Castlereagh wrote (March 7th): "We have against us 120 M.P.'s, well combined and united, many of them of the first weight and talent in the House; 37 of them are members for counties. Dublin is almost unanimous against it." According to the "Cornwallis Correspondence," "every despatch written during the last eighteen months fully apprised the English ministers that the

[1] Alison's "Life of Castlereagh," vol. i. p. 105.
[2] Ibid. vol. i. pp. 109-112.
[3] "Cornwallis Correspondence," vol. iii. p. 177.

measure could only be carried by influence. £1,260,000 was ultimately awarded for seats lost, &c. Lord Downshire got £52,500 for seven; Lord Ely, £45,000." [1]

Lord Cornwallis had been "the person to buy out and secure to the Crown for ever the fee-simple of Irish corruption. It would have been fatal to the measure if the objections, or even the disinclination of ministers to any professed arrangement, had transpired." [2]

When Castlereagh either feared or found that the king would not grant the consideration on which Catholics had agreed to the union, he wrote a strong remonstrance to Pitt, in which the following occurs—that the statement he had personally made to Pitt was that "the majority was of very doubtful materials, the Protestants badly divided, and the Dublin and Orange societies against us, the Catholics holding back; that the measure could not be carried if they embarked in active opposition, and that their resistance would be unanimous and zealous"—without the expected concession—because "the union itself might give ministers additional means of disappointing their hopes. I stated that attempts had been made by leading Catholics to bring Government to an explanation, which had of course been evaded. That the friends of Government, by flattering the hopes of the Catholics, had produced a favourable impression in Cork, Tipperary, and Galway. That his Excellency was enabled to accomplish his purpose without direct assurances to Catholics, but foresaw the awkward circumstances to which the transaction was likely to lead." [3]

In the following month (February 7th), the king himself wrote to the Hon. Henry Dundas:

---

[1] "Cornwallis Correspondence," vol. iii. pp. 266, 323, 324.

[2] Lord Castlereagh to Mr. Cooke, June 21 and 25, 1800. "Cornwallis Correspondence," vol. iii. p. 267.

[3] Castlereagh to Pitt, January 1, 1801. "Castlereagh Correspondence," vol. iv. pp. 8, 12.

"I cannot but regret that I had not been treated with more confidence previous to forming an opinion which, to my greatest surprise, I learned on Thursday from Earl Spencer, has been in agitation ever since Lord Castlereagh came over in August, yet of which I never had the smallest suspicion till within these very few weeks; but so desirous was I to avoid the present conclusion, that except . . . I have been silent on the subject, and, indeed, hoping that Mr. Pitt had not pledged himself on what I cannot with my sentiments of religious and political duty think myself at liberty to concur." [1]

To get out of this dilemma, Pitt resigned on February 5, 1801, and Lord Castlereagh privately wrote that Pitt had proceeded in favour of the Catholics, thinking the king's mind would not give way, but that now during his life there was no hope.[2] On the 12th the king's mental alienation became decided, his symptoms not being so much those of entire derangement as of mental oppression and anxiety, which often found relief in tears.[3]

George III., in answer to Pitt's recommendation in letter January 31, 1801, that "Catholics and Dissenters be admitted to offices, and Catholics to parliament," pleaded his coronation oath and sacramental obligation to the contrary:

"My inclination to a union with Ireland was principally founded on a trust that the uniting the Established Churches of the two kingdoms would for ever shut the door to any further measures with respect to the Roman Catholics." [4]

The king also wrote of the

"Fundamental maxims on which the Constitution is placed; namely, the Church of England being the established one, that

[1] "Cornwallis Correspondence," vol. iii. p. 333.
[2] "Castlereagh Correspondence," vol. iv. pp. 39, 40.
[3] All Geo. III.'s published letters on this subject are at the appendices of Stanhope's five volumes on Pitt.
[4] Stanhope's Pitt, vol. ii. appendix.

those who hold employment in the State must be members of it, and, consequently, obliged not only to take oaths against popery, but to receive the holy communion agreeably to the rites of the Church of England."

"The king's mind," said Earl Russell in his letter (1868) to Mr. Fortescue :

"Had been poisoned by his Chancellor, Lord Loughborough, and influenced by the authority of the Archbishop of Canterbury; and their opinions had been brought to weigh upon the king's decision by artful intrigues before the large and wise view of Mr. Pitt had been allowed to reach him.

"Besides the fury of the Irish Protestants, maddened by the fear that their monopoly was in danger, Mr. Pitt had to persuade George III. Nine years afterwards, my father, returning from Ireland where he had held the office of Lord-Lieutenant, had an audience of the king, but representing that the admission of Roman Catholics to the office of sheriff would give confidence, the king got into so violent a state of excitement, that my father was obliged to desist. It is an alliance thus made, cemented by cruelty, violence, and corruption, which is now said to be so sacred that no tittle of it can be altered without sacrilege and robbery !"

At the close of 1799 Grattan returned from the Isle of Wight almost broken-hearted, but in mind unsubdued. Immediately a deputation pressed him to enter parliament, but he declined. Soon after there was a death vacancy, but Grattan said he would be no party to the union which was an act of suicide. Mrs. Grattan—Henrietta Grattan —whose narrative I follow, urged him to take the seat— that he ought to spend his money or shed his blood for the people.

"Unable to bear noise, we avoided hotels and went to Mr. Austen's, in Dublin, to await the election, which, the sheriff being friendly, was managed after 12 o'clock on the night of the 15th of January, 1800, the last session of the Dublin Parliament. At five o'clock in the morning Mr. Tighe arrived on horseback in

Dublin, and we heard loud knocking. Grattan was ill in bed and said, 'Why will they not let me die in peace?' He grew quite wild. I told him he must go to the House, and helped him downstairs, when he went into the parlour and loaded his pistols, for he apprehended assassination by the Union party. We wrapped a blanket round him in the sedan chair, and I stood at the door uncertain whether I should ever see him again. Mr. M'Can said that Grattan's friends had determined to come forward if he were attacked. I said, 'My husband cannot die better than in defence of his country.'"

Then came Sir L. Parsons' amendment and the debate.

"At 7 o'clock in the morning Grattan entered. He could scarcely walk, and was supported on either side. Ministers were not aware that the writ could have been returned. The House and galleries were breathless, and a thrilling sensation, a low murmur pervaded the whole assembly, as this emaciated figure, sick in mind and body—the founder, eighteen years before, of Ireland's independence—now came forward, apparently almost in his last moments, to defend or fall with his country. His friends crowded round to assist. Bowes Daly, seeing he had his hat on, mentioned it. 'Don't mind me,' said Grattan, 'I know what to do.' He was dressed, this soldier of '82, in the volunteer uniform —blue, with red cuffs and collar. He had placed his cocked hat square to the front, till he advanced half way up the floor. He then stopped and looked round the House as one prepared for battle; then approached the table, took off his hat, took the oath, and his seat, and as Mr. Egan sat down Grattan rose, and, obtaining leave to speak sitting, to the astonishment of every one, spoke for upwards of two hours, going through the whole question."[1]

This great speech proved incontestably that:

"The one great, capital, fundamental cause of Irish discontent was the interposition of the Parliament of Great Britain in the legislative regulation of Ireland, the interference of that or any other parliament, save only the King, Lords, and Commons of Ireland.

[1] "Grattan's Life and Times."

The minister denies, in the face of the two nations, a public fact registered and recorded, and he disclaims the final adjustment of 1782.

"The Parliament of Ireland have ever since their emancipation concurred with England on the subject of war; but before their concurrence was barren, since it has been productive. In 1783 they voted a sum for British seamen, and on the apprehension of a war with Spain, in 1790, they voted another, and in the present war, a third. So much more beneficial are the wild offerings of liberty than the squeezings, and eviscerations, and excruciations of power.

"Ireland considers the British Empire a great western barrier against invasion from other countries.

"She hears the ocean protesting against separation, but she hears the sea likewise protesting against union; she follows therefore her physical destination, and obeys the dispensations of providence when she protests, like that sea, against the two situations, both equally unnatural—separation and union; but then she feels her Constitution to be her great stake in the empire, and the empire the great security of her Constitution. We give our strength to this western barrier for the security of our liberty; but if British ministers should do that very mischief which we apprehend from the foreigner, namely, take away the Constitution, they take away with that our interest in the British dominions, and thus withdraw at once a great pillar of liberty and empire.

"That Constitution has been the inheritance of this country for six hundred years. The Constitution the minister destroys is the condition of our connection; he destroys one of the pillars of the British Empire—the habitation of Irish loyalty. I say of her loyalty as well as her liberty, her temple of fame as well as of freedom, where she had seated herself, as she vainly thought, in modest security and a long repose."[1]

"Well, the minister has destroyed the Constitution. To destroy is easy. The edifices of the mind, like the fabrics of marble, require an age to build, but ask only minutes to precipitate; and, as the fall of both is of no time, so neither is it a business of any

---

[1] "Tract." Jordan, Fleet Street. 1800: "Grattan's Speeches." Edited by his son. Longman, 1822.

strength. A pickaxe and a common labourer will do the one, a little lawyer, a little pimp, and a wicked minister the other. . . .

" I have done with the pile which the minister batters. I come to the Babel which he builds, and as he throws down without a principle, so does he construct without a foundation. This fabric he calls a union. It is no union, for it excludes the Catholics. It is an extinction of the Constitution, and an exclusion of the people. He has overlooked the people, as he has overlooked the sea.

"I affirm that the blessings procured by the Irish Parliament in the last twenty years are greater than all the blessings afforded by British Parliaments to Ireland for the last century, greater even than the mischiefs inflicted on Ireland by the British Parliament.

" He, the minister, 'his budget with corruption crammed,' proposes to you to give up the ancient inheritance of your country, to proclaim an utter and blank incapacity to make laws for your own people, and to register their proclamation in an act which inflicts on this ancient nation an eternal disability, and he accompanies these monstrous proposals by undisguised terror and unqualified bribery."

At ten in the morning the House divided; majority against amendment and Grattan, 42.

On the 21st of January, 1800, Castlereagh proposed that 10,000 volunteers from the Irish militia should serve in Europe at a large bounty; and that English militia should take their place.

On February 5th the union question was brought on, and Lord Castlereagh, in proposing resolutions in favour of union, made it evident that the maintenance of the Irish Church Establishment was one great object of the union. He said :

" There would be no possibility of giving the Irish Church Establishment security in any other way than by a complete incorporation with that of Great Britain. While the present system continued one minister might wish to uphold the present Establishment, another the system of exclusion, and a third to open the Establishment to every claimant. Under such a policy the country would never be quiet. But the Establishment being incorporated, the Protestant would feel himself supported," &c.

On that occasion Grattan declared:

"The question is not now such as occupied you of old—not old Poyning's, not peculation, not plunder, not an embargo, not a Catholic Bill, not a Reform Bill—it is your being, it is your life to come."

The majority against Grattan was 43.

Corry then for the third time attacked Grattan personally, but this time Grattan—who said to Foster, "I see they wish to make an attack on my life, and the sooner the better"—could reply, and his reply electrified, almost appalled, the House. There in the hall of his former glories, amidst the dying embers of his country's freedom, he strove to snatch from the sacred pile a brand that might light her to resurrection! He arraigned the Government; they conspired against the country; they were corrupt and seditious; they sold themselves, and they sold the Constitution. Two parties were in arms against the country—the rebel who deserved to die, and the right honourable gentleman whom he missed from the scaffold.

"I have returned to protect that Constitution of which I was the parent and the founder from the assassination of such men as the right honourable gentleman and his unworthy associates. They are corrupt, they are seditious, and they at this moment are in a conspiracy against their country. . . . I dare accusation. I defy the honourable gentleman. I defy the Government. I defy their whole phalanx; let them come forth. I tell the ministers I will neither give them quarter nor take it."[1]

On May 26th Grattan thus brought up the climax:

"The Constitution may for a time be lost, but liberty may

[1] "Life and Times," vol. v. pp. 103, 104.

repair her golden beams, and with redoubled heart animate the country. I see her in a swoon, but she is not dead—

> 'Thou art not conquered; beauty's ensign yet
> Is crimson in thy lips, and in thy cheeks;
> And death's pale flag is not advancèd there.'"

On the 6th of June, 1800, a protest of twelve closely printed pages was presented against the union, but the majority for the union was 58.

Lord Castlereagh then moved that the Bill be engrossed. Mr. O'Donnell moved as amendment, "that the Bill be burned;" and Colonel Tighe added, "by the common hangman." Twenty-four Irish peers protested against the union, but the Act passed on the 1st of January, 1801 (40 Geo. III., c. 67).[1]

[1] In "Grattan's Life and Times," vol. v. pp. 188–196, are the original "red and black lists" of 150 and 140 respectively, showing those members of parliament who could and could not be corrupted by Castlereagh, and what the former got for their votes; wherefrom it is evident that 25 were purchased shortly before the second division in 1800, making a difference of 50.

The appendix to the last volume also contains the protests of Irish lords against the union, and that drawn up and moved in the Commons.

NATIONAL RESURRECTION.

> "Thou art not conquered; beauty's ensign yet
> Is crimson in thy lips, and in thy cheeks;
> And death's pale flag is not advancèd there."
> —*Quoted by* GRATTAN.

"Grattan sat by the cradle of his country, and followed her hearse; it was left for me to sound the resurrection trumpet, and to show that she was not dead, but sleeping."—O'CONNELL.

"The angels of martyrdom and of victory are brothers; but it is only when from epoch to epoch their eyes meet between heaven and earth, that creation is embellished with a new life, and a people arises, evangelist or prophet, from the cradle or the tomb."—MAZZINI.

"But I go back to the consideration of the great question of national self-government for Ireland. We cannot ask for less than the restitution of Grattan's Parliament with its important privileges, and wide and far-reaching Constitution."—MR. PARNELL *at Cork, January* 21, 1885.

"The connection with England thus becomes the cause of the present state of Ireland. If the connection with England prevents a revolution, and a revolution is the only remedy, England logically is in the odious position of being the cause of all the misery in Ireland. What, then, is the duty of an English minister? To effect by his policy all those changes which revolution would do by force. That is the Irish question in its integrity."—D'ISRAELI, *February* 16, 1844.

"To this act of union must be attributed the three famines since 1800, with their million and a half of deaths, the exile of nearly three millions of Irishmen, and in eighty-five years three rebellions and eighty-four Coercion Bills."—T. P. O'CONNOR, M.P., *The Parnell Movement*.

"New and terrible diseases sprang up; children were growing idiots.... a new race with only a distant and hideous resemblance to humanity. I saw these accursed sights, and they are burned into my memory for ever. Poor, mutilated, debased scions, of a tender, brave, and pious stock—martyrs in the battle of centuries for the right to live in their own land."—THE HON. C. GAVAN DUFFY, *on the results of Pitt's masterpiece*.

"When numbers, means, and opposition are considered, the Parnell testimonial equals, or more than equals, that raised for Cobden. The desire for nationality is at the root of Irish discontent. Home Rule means improved union. When there are already eighteen independent parliaments in the British dominions, it is only prejudice to contend that another would make the difference between union and dismemberment."—JOSEPH COWEN, M.P., 1883.

"I still retain my opinion that Mr. Gladstone, encountering great risks, and provoking bitter animosity, has aimed at the welfare of his country in the mighty struggle in which he has engaged. If he should aspire to perform a permanent and immortal service to his country, to reconcile England and Ireland, then indeed he will be enrolled among the noblest of England's statesmen. I feel sure Mr. Gladstone will not propose to take a leap in the dark. The wreath *ob civem servatum* will be a million times deserved by the minister who shall knit together three nations."—EARL RUSSELL, 1869.

"I ask you to examine the state of Her Majesty's Government for the last thirty-five years. From 1794 there has been disunion in the Government on account of the Catholic question, and the administration of Irish affairs. The consequences have been most unfavourable to the administration of the affairs of this country (England). The Cabinets have in general been equally divided ; . . . jealousies, suspicions between honourable men.

"Let us now turn to the legislature. Each party can paralyze the other. . . . But what becomes of Ireland if these party conflicts without a result shall continue? For scarcely one year since the Union has Ireland been governed by the ordinary course of law."—SIR R. PEEL, *on Results of the Union, March* 5, 1829. Hansard.

"The manner in which and the terms upon which Mr. Pitt effected the union, made it the most fatal blow ever levelled against the peace and prosperity of England."—S. T. COLERIDGE, 1831.

"This nation was to reap marvellous blessings from the Union ; but of what benefit is the junction of four or five millions of traitors—such as I tell you they are not—a grosser outrage upon truth, a greater libel upon a generous people, never before was uttered ! Sir ! I love the Irish nation. There is not one feature more predominant than gratitude and sensibility to kindness. Change your system towards that country, and you will find them another sort of men. Let impartiality, justice, clemency, take the place of prejudice, oppression, and vengeance, and you will not want the aid of martial law."—FOX's *Speeches*, v. 6, p. 448.

NATIONAL RESURRECTION.

CHAPTER IV.

THE COMMERCIAL, NATIONAL, AND IMPERIAL BANKRUPTCY OF THE UNION;

AND THE

NATIONAL RESURRECTION.

O'Connell, — Parnell, — Gladstone.

"The landlords' power has been increased exceedingly since 1800. The supply of land is not equal to the demand. The tenant is obliged to take the land at any price. If things go on as they do, murders will accumulate, and fixity of tenure will be conquered from the landlord by fear. Before 1800 no power to eject, except, &c. Since 1800 power of selling and distraining growing crops was given. I don't think there is anything in nature by which greater oppression can be practised. By seizure nothing is left to subsist on. If he digs he is sent to gaol, and his family left to starve. The wilful trespass act gives a frightful dominion to the landlord class, maddening stimulants to crime."—DANIEL O'CONNELL'S *evidence before Devon Commission*, 1845.

"A landlord of straw can grind to powder a tenant of steel."—LORD CLARE.

"The land question contains, and the legislative question does not contain, the materials from which victory is to be manufactured. Victory follows that banner and no other. There can be no right of property in eight thousand against the property, security, independence, and existence, of eight millions—to take their food and give them famine, to take their home and give them the workhouse. Such rights are the code of the brigand, and can be enforced only by the hangman."—JAMES FINTAN LALOR, *in The Irish Felon*, 1848.

"The principle I state, and mean to stand upon, is this—that the entire ownership of Ireland, moral and material, body, land, and soul, up to the sun and down to the centre, is vested of right in the people of Ireland. The entire soil of a country belongs of right to the entire people. I will put Ireland in the van of the world, and set her aloft in the blaze of the sun."—*Ibid.*

"I have done with the pile which the minister batters; I come to the Babel which he builds."—GRATTAN.

FROM Molyneux, Swift, Flood, Grattan, and Sheil, to

Parnell and Gladstone, we see, first, the dawn of national self-consciousness, the beginning of the making of the Irish nation, and the drawing together of its elemental powers—consecrated from 1770 to 1800 to one prolonged supreme endeavour after national life; next, the apparent sudden arrest, but real concentration and exasperation of all these factors and forces by Pitt, the unmaker, the divider, the undoer, the deceiver, the destroyer, and the destroyed; then the first great national victory since the Union, under O'Connell; the establishment of a national propagandism and organ by C. Gavan Duffy, and the men of *The Nation* in 1843; the fusion of the land and nation questions by James Fintan Lalor, in *The Irish Felon* of 1848; the disendowment of a Protestant sect by Gladstone; the establishment of an Irish party of action in the English House; the Anglo-Irish-American-Australian agitation amongst the ten millions, started by Davitt and Parnell; and now the coming restoration of the land and nation to itself, the crowning of the edifice by Gladstone—the resurrection blast for Ireland, and Pitt's day of judgment.

What has happened is that Pitt with his mechanics challenged nature and destiny, with the usual result. He saw well enough the separate forces with whose jealousies he calculated on dividing and conquering, namely, the English garrison Church, the Irish landlord junto, the Orangemen and the Roman Catholics; but he forgot to reckon with George III. and the Irish nation, and the first stultified him whilst the last has extinguished him. If it be true that the only deadly, unpardonable sin of nations is not to revolt against injustice, Ireland has not committed that sin; if it be true that the unpardonable sin of statesmen is to attempt to destroy a nation, that sin Pitt is guilty of. The fault of Pitt's policy, as a policy, was not that it was not wicked enough, but that it was too wicked in this part of the world to spread or to last. He ought also to have been able to corrupt, enslave, or destroy, and that for ever, the moral sense of England.

By instructing Lords Cornwallis and Castlereagh to persuade the Catholics of that which he, Mr. Pitt, knew to be untrue, or did not know to be true, namely, that their emancipation would accompany the Union, he could just carry the Union—which he did at the cost of the poor honest king's reason, and of the personal honour of all concerned, Lord Cornwallis confessing[1] that most of the bought votes in the House would be only too delighted if they were voted down.

Pitt, however, had to reckon with another enemy, neither mortal nor gullible—the Irish nation. Pitt never saw this: Pitts don't. Statesmen go, and kings and cabinets with them, but nations remain and are eternal. Pitt's foe was as indestructible as the poor king's honesty, and as is Pitt's dishonour. It was the alpha and omega, the first and the last and the whole of Ireland. It is to-day trampling under foot all that is left of Pitt and his policy. What Pitt defied was the only primordial, indestructible force in Ireland, namely, Ireland herself; and granted that fact and time—the rest was destiny.

Pitt's "Union"—the concentrated essence of all trickery, folly, falsehood, and disunion—was forsooth to checkmate the nation—God's work and nature's stronghold. There remains now of the Union and of Pitt, poor histrio! only his bagful of tricks found out, his "emancipation" marked card, his properties, stage effects, and pretences, a century of vengeful memories, an imperishable contempt, and a certain Act of Parliament which never acted.

> "The painted jay comes smirking down the tree,
> Like a gay gallant from a ruined maiden."

The Act of Union was, in fact, what would have been termed later, "a Slave State Extension Act." A preserve

[1] See "Cornwallis Correspondence."

was wanted off the English coast, where the king's writ should overrun as many of the ten commandments as were inconvenient to the minority, just as another preserve was wanted lately in the American "Territories" for another felon flag to fly on. Pitt and Castlereagh's minority struck under cover of religion and law, and plea of tender conscience, by bailiffs and agents, and by statutes passed four hundred miles away.

The Union was, as we have seen, essential to the continuance of the Irish Protestant Establishment, which in the aggregate United Kingdom electorate was no longer a minority Church. The Union was also immediately used, as it was meant to be used, to enormously increase landlord power, and laws were enacted scarcely possible in a national parliament, to set the tenant naked and shelterless before all the blasts that blow, until even Lord Clare confessed that "a landlord of straw could grind to powder a tenant of steel." It was this very injustice that enabled the Irish leaders, later, to link together in propagandism Irish nationality and land, in order to free the one and make the other; an attempt which, succeeding, will emerge to the equal advantage of the English and Irish nations and the Britannic Empire.

We have to consider how the factors of Irish legislative independence accumulated, whilst Whig and Tory nostrums failed to keep the two nations, with their great ideas of union, justice, peace, aggregate strength, and empire, entirely in the background.

The key to the situation has been the gradual and real "union" of the Irish people amongst themselves, inspirited and led by O'Connell, *The Nation*, Lalor, Davitt, and Parnell, and supported by the Irish emigration, and the advantage which the English parliamentary system gives to agitation as a science of progress. We have witnessed Catholic emancipation which destroyed the greatest enemy of national union, and are witnessing the emancipation of the land. We see even now the representatives of the great Whig Protestant junto, which formerly commanded 116 Irish members of parliament, discredited, left out, and left behind; whilst the statesmanship of common sense and international morality stimulates and shares the irresistible advance of the principle of Irish nationality.

The Irish nation had found a voice, had had an army, controlled its own revenue, knew what it wanted, and was proceeding to unite and enfranchise its citizens, who would then free its trade, Church, and land. This did not suit Pitt, whose ruling minority in Ireland would have been destroyed by it. The only plan to keep things as they were—the Establishment up and the nation down—was to swamp the Irish electorate with the English, to remove its representatives from Ireland, to separate the bane, bad government, from the antidote, public opinion, by hundreds of miles, and, as it has turned out, a century of time.

The century has gone; Pitt's day of judgment has come and gone too, and nothing but the nation and its future remains.

The history of this one hundred years is the history of the preservation of everything Pitt tried to paralyze and corrupt, and of the paralysis and destruction of all he tried to establish. Where is the Irish minority Church? Where is the Protestant landlords junto? What has been the discipline, subordination, and union of "the Union"? What its help to the empire? Where is his Protestant ascendency?

"The fierce and infinite laugh at things that cease"—

has long since answered these questions. It only now remains to sweep away Pitt and all his lumber into the everlasting dustbin.

Lord Holland says, "The fact is incontrovertible that the

people of Ireland were driven to resistance by the free quarters and excesses of the soldiery, which were such as are not permitted in civilized warfare, even in an enemy's country."[1]

Sir Ralph Abercrombie, who knew well, stated respecting the army in Ireland, that "it was in a state of licentiousness which must render it formidable to every one but the enemy. The Government were the jealous and watchful advocates of military rule, and of the uncontrolled license of the troops."[2]

"The Irish Government in 1798 might have crushed the rebellion, but they let it go on on purpose to carry the Union, and that was their design. One letter in particular showed their duplicity. When Lord Clonmel was dying, he stated this to Dean Scott and made him destroy the letter. He further added that he had told the lieutenant that as they knew the proceedings of the disaffected, it was wrong to permit them to go on, but should crush them and prevent the insurrection. He was coldly received. Lord Clare's advice predominated, and in consequence he, Lord Clonmel, was not summoned to (future) Privy Councils on business of State."[3]

With a national or any electorate that understood the matter, the frightful landlord legislation which followed the Union would have been simply impossible. These laws[4] involved cheapened ejectment and a lower class of tenant; shortened notice of process; possible distress or ejectment by paramount landlord for rent already paid; destruction of all sacredness of possession; legal and unjust eviction for want of stamps on agreement; the sale and distraint of growing crops, the daily food of the peasant, who had to starve or "rescue distress;" and the wilful trespass Act, which annihilated all the smaller rights of the peasant.

[1] "Memoirs of the Whig Party." Longmans, 1852.
[2] Memoir, by his son, p. 93.
[3] "Grattan's Life and Times," vol. ii. pp. 145-6.
[4] See O'Connell's evidence, Devon Commission.

The only benefits which the Union conferred on England were those which men like Pitt abominate. They were conferred by the co-operation of Irish representatives with the English party of progress in the English House, and are recorded by the great antagonist of his policy, O'Connell, in that most faithful and pathetic memoir addressed by him to the Queen:

" I desire these four facts to be remembered :

" 1st. That the Irish representatives turned the scale of victory, and carried the English Parliamentary Reform Bill.

" 2nd. They equally, and by the same act, carried the Scotch Reform Bill.

" 3rd. They equally, and by inevitable consequence, carried the English Municipal Reform Bill.

" 4th. They equally carried the Scotch Municipal Reform Bill" (p. 34).

"Illustrious Lady, the rebellion of 1798 itself was almost avowedly, and beyond a doubt probably, fomented to enable the British Government to extinguish the Irish legislative independence, and to bring about the Union" (p. 26).

"We feel and understand that if the Union was not in existence, if Ireland had her own parliament, the popular majority would have long since carried every measure of salutary and useful reform. Instead of being behindhand with England and Scotland, we should have taken the lead, and achieved for ourselves all and more than we have contributed to achieve for them.

"If there were no Union, Ireland would be the part of the British dominions in which greater progress would have been made in civil and religious liberty than in any other part, subject to the British Crown. If the Union had not been carried, Ireland would have long since paid off her national debt, and been now almost entirely freely from taxation.

"The Union, and the Union alone, stands in the way of our achieving for ourselves every political blessing.

" Injustice, degradation, comparative weakness, widespread poverty, unendurable political inferiority—these are the fruits of the Union. . . .

"Upon a population of eight millions, there are two millions three hundred thousand individuals dependent for subsistence on casual charity !!! And this in one of the most abundantly fertile countries on the globe !" (p. 39).

Yes, this is the crowning test of that wonderful prosperity which men disloyal to Ireland, and patriotic against their own country, now allege to have followed the Union —more than a fourth of the population paupers !

As though rational men require to have it argued that a trade of Irish cattle and produce to England, stimulated by the high prices of the French war, whilst Irish western harbours were kept empty and Irish peasants starving, was no proof of prosperity; as if it were possible that a dependent country, exploited by an alien, irresponsible, dominant oligarchy, could be, or would be allowed to be, benefited thereby !

These extra-patriotic and loyal gentlemen prove too much. If their nation was really so uneasy under such unbounded prosperity as to want a Coercion Act every year, what were they uneasy about ? Not about material prosperity. That, it seems, they had ; no, it must have been their intense yearnings after national existence that made them scorn the Whig manna and the Tory honey spread for them in the wilderness of the Union, that made them turn with loathing from the fat pastures of Castlereagh, and the flesh-pots of Pitt and Peel, and strain their eyes towards the promised land of independence, and the *Zion* of nationality they had left !

An Irish National Debt raised from two or three millions to £150,000,000 in seventeen years of union, is a further proof—if any more were wanted—of its wonder-working advantages !

As early as the 19th of March, 1811, Sir John Newport, in the English House, moved three resolutions :

1. "That the funded debt of Ireland had trebled within ten years, and was on the 5th of January, 1811, £89,208,000, occa-

sioning an annual permanent charge for interest, sinking fund, and management of £4,273,000; and that the ordinary revenue of Ireland had been last year only £3,614,000."

Nothing came of this, or of the other resolutions, but a committee and an elaborate report.

Before the Union, and under the superintendence of a national resident Parliament, the debt of the nation had diminished from £2,477,423 in 1789, to £2,219,694 in 1793. In 1799, when the Union had for some years been determined on, and Pitt's Viceroys had begun to carry out his system of corruption, the debt was thirteen millions, and in 1800 twenty-four millions. In 1814 it was 116 millions, and in 1817 it became bankrupt, and the debts and exchequers were consolidated. After that the Irish revenue for forty years rather declined than otherwise, for in 1803 it was £4,337,269, in 1804 £3,717,942, and in 1841 £4,107,066.[1]

Since the Union, the minister found it necessary to establish a force of 10,000 armed police, and a regular army of 20,000 and upwards in time of peace. As to destitution and pauperism, the Commissioners of the Land Inquiry of 1845 reported that "a large proportion of the entire population comes within the designation of agricultural labourers, and endure sufferings greater than those of the people of any other country in Europe." Prior to that report, the commissioners, in the railway report laid before Parliament, stated that the number of destitute persons found annually in Ireland amounted to 2,300,000.[2]

In 1816 distress was rapidly increasing throughout Ireland. The general decline of manufactures was aggravated by the absence of the nobility and gentry from Dublin, and even its citizens became almost unable to pay ordinary taxes. The evil consequences of the Union were spreading, and national bankruptcy approaching. In

[1] "Grattan's Life and Times," vol. v. pp. 181, 187.
[2] Ibid. vol. v. p. 187.

April Sir John Newport proposed an address to the Prince Regent, depicting the poverty and distress, the civil and religious discord, Catholics excluded, Orangemen supported by the Government.

In the debate Mr. Plunket said that soon 40,000 soldiers would be required in Ireland. Mr. Grattan said that her debt was £150,000,000, her interest above £6,000,000, her revenue £5,000,000.

Peel, who was Irish Secretary from 1813 to 1819, evaded the motion, but bankruptcy could not be evaded. The Chancellor could not collect the assessed taxes, and even in the North of Ireland—the wealthiest part—notices were served that carriages, horses, servants, cars, &c., would be given up—3,000 notices of this sort in one year.

On the 20th of May resolutions were submitted by the Chancellor, of which the third was "that the annual revenue of Great Britain and Ireland be consolidated."

Mr. Leslie Foster, afterwards one of the Barons of Exchequer, said that Ireland's contributions these fifteen years were £103,000,000, and the whole amount of available revenue in that period was £12,735,000. The Union imposed an expenditure on Ireland eight times greater than her revenue. In nine years Irish taxes had doubled; in 1800, £2,440,000; in 1816, £5,752,000.[1]

"It is to be observed that in 1785, when the British manufacturers formed their committee in England, the evidence stated that if the Irish continued their exertions they would rival the British in foreign markets; as a remedy, they asked for a union —and the decay of Ireland followed."[2]

"What the island chiefly produced was food, which was exported to richer countries to enable the cultivator to pay an inordinate rent; harbours looking towards the East were occupied only by ships which carried raw produce and human food to England. The food of the peasant was potatoes, with a little milk

---

[1] "Grattan's Life and Times," vol. v. pp. 525-7-8.
[2] Ibid. vol. v. p. 98.

or salt; flesh meat he rarely tasted. The country was famous for the production of butter, and the growth of beef and mutton, and especially of pork; but butter, beef, mutton, and pork were nearly as unknown as an article of diet among the peasantry as among the Hindoos."[1]

It is the exportation of this cattle, &c., away from the peasantry to England, "to enable them to pay an inordinate rent," which shows how well off these peasants must have been! *Risum teneatis!* The same sort of logic that proved the Irish were not hungry, might have been used with as great advantage to show that Tantalus was never thirsty.

The sudden paralysis of intellectual, parliamentary, social, and commercial life inflicted by the Union on Dublin, affected the whole nation:

"The prosperity of Dublin prior to the Union partook in far more than a proportionate degree of the rapid advances which Ireland made in population, commerce, civilization, and literature, in the latter half of the eighteenth century, and yet more particularly at the period of legislative independence. Within that half-century all the public institutions of utility or elegance, all those embellishments and improvements which still exist, were completed or commenced. The reason of the decline is sufficiently obvious. Prior to the Union, between four and five hundred families of rank and opulence, residents, are no longer to be found in Dublin. London, that overgrown and bloated capitol, absorbs all the wealth and talents of the sister metropolis and kingdom."[2]

In Sir H. Parnell's able work on "Financial Reform"[3] are given (appendix 8) tables which show undoubted apparent prosperity in Ireland from 1790 to 1826. But he adds to them (pp. 259-60-63) the statement, that

"It may be long before the condition of the labouring class will become much better than it now (1832) is—wages not keep-

---

[1] See "Young Ireland," pp. 139, 141.
[2] Whitelaw and Walsh, 1818.
[3] Murray, 1832. 4th edition.

ing pace with the price of food. . . . Industry and accumulation of wealth must have been greatly obstructed by agitation. Malthus remarks with great force, that among the most important causes that influence the wealth of nations must be placed politics and morals. Security of property depends upon the political constitution and administration. But the law which deprived several millions of Catholics in Ireland of their civil rights, established hostility to laws and general discontent. Ireland's opportunities have been thrown away. From 1802 to 1816, the demand for her productions was so great and the prices so high with reference to the cost of production, that had it not been for the defect in her political and moral condition, she must have become a very rich and flourishing country. Had she possessed free and tolerant laws, and the same habits, as England, Scotland, Holland, Switzerland, and the United States, an immense accumulation of wealth would have been secured before the fall of prices which took place subsequent to 1816."

The official tables quoted by Sir H. Parnell show that the annual average amount of the imports and exports of Ireland for the triennial periods ending as follows, were:

	Imports.	Exports.
1790	£3,535,588	£4,125,333.
1800	£4,299,493	£4,015,976.
1810	£6,535,068	£5,270,471.
1820	£6,008,273	£6,291,275.
1826	£7,491,890	£8,454,918.

But the question is, how many of the good things implied in the doubling of imports and exports, even in thirty-six years, were enjoyed by the people themselves? and Sir H. Parnell's tables showing the articles " retained for home consumption " during the same period in Ireland are very precise and full, and of far more consequence than those inconsequential figures supplied by the " loyal and patriotic" statisticians of the present hour. I take only three principal articles:

	Tea (lbs.)	Coffee (lbs.)	Sugar (cwts.)
1790	1,732,374	44,370	216,106.
1800	2,773,070	73,262	241,224.
1820	3,316,321	405,186	317,833.
1826	3,548,293	277,465	406,789.

The ratio of advance in the articles retained for the people's own use is nothing like that of cattle, &c., sent abroad. One of the reasons was that the artificial prices caused by the war, ceased with it. The rents raised by war prices were not reduced when war prices fell. The population was then six millions, and had to compete for land, and a policy little short of extermination was revived. Peel was Irish Secretary, and a new constabulary force was organized in 1815, and also a series of cheap ejectment Acts. Moreover, in 1816, a committee to inquire into the state of Ireland was moved for, but successfully resisted by Peel. An inquiry would have revealed starvation, and reform might have been substituted for coercion.

Pitt had poisoned the well-springs of Anglo-Irish national life. He slackened the bonds and palsied the power of empire; he dissolved the Irish social system; he has been the Mephistopheles of the Irish assassin and of the Irish landlord, presenting the one with a reduced rent roll, and the other with a loaded blunderbuss and landlord law; his iron entered into the soul of the peasantry, making vengeance and despair their familiar spirit. He slaughtered 150,000 of those who asked only to be most loyal subjects on the face of the earth; he broke the spirit of a noble people, and kept the Catholic question sweltering for thirty-five years.

"The union," wrote O'Connell, "entitled the Catholics of Ireland—that is, emphatically the people of Ireland—to religious equality with the English and Scotch. It was thus distinctly, and in writing, avowed by Pitt in his negotiation with Catholic peers and others who called themselves the leaders of the Catholic people." [1]

Pitt bought the Irish birthright for the price of emancipation, and then did not emancipate; as Mr. Lecky says, "Lords Cornwallis and Castlereagh had purchased the support of the leading Catholic prelates by a distinct intimation that in their opinion the union would be a prelude to emancipation." Pitt's Irish policy was a gigantic confidence trick all round, played not in a tavern, but with empire. He befooled one people and their sovereign that he might abscond with the nationality and parliament of another. He misled the king, tricked the Irish people, dissimulated with the Irish landlords, and used and partly deceived Castlereagh. He nearly murdered his sovereign and Ireland.

These two, religion and nationality, the one the greatest force in Ireland, the other the greatest force in the universe, Pitt elected to combine against a union which was not a union, and which was based only on corruption and physical force.

Pitt directly caused the rebellion by the peremptory recall of Fitzwilliam. As Mr. Lecky remarks:

"A careful examination will show that at every period of Pitt's career he sacrificed or subordinated political principles to party ends. The steady object of his later Irish policy was to corrupt and to degrade, in order that he might ultimately destroy the legislature of the country; and he was guilty in Ireland of a system of corruption before which the worst acts of Newcastle and Walpole dwindle into insignificance. The rebellion of 1798, with all the accumulated miseries it entailed, was the direct and predicted consequence of Pitt's policy.[2] Ireland in 1795 was singularly easy to govern, had it been governed honestly and by honest men. Pitt sowed in Ireland the seeds of discord and bloodshed, of religious animosities, and social disorganization,

[1] Memoir, p. 40.
[2] "Lecky on Grattan," p. 147, edition 1871.

which paralyzed the energies of the country, and rendered possible the success of his machinations."

In his letter, October 7, 1784, to the Duke of Rutland, Lord-lieutenant, he wrote:

"I own to you the line to which my mind at present inclines is to give Ireland an almost unlimited communication of commercial advantages, if we can receive some security that her strength and riches will be for our benefit; to be ready, by acceding to a prudent and temperate reform of parliament, . . . and may unite the Protestant interest in excluding the Catholics from any share in the representation or government of the country."

In another unpublished letter, January 6, 1785, Pitt remarks that local advantages should be relinquished for the general benefit of the empire; and "this cannot be done but by making England and Ireland one country in effect, though for local concerns under distinct legislatures."[1]

But Pitt was vexed and offended with the conduct of Ireland in 1785 on the commercial propositions, and in 1789 on the Regency, when, as O'Connell has said, he wanted to make himself the virtual king. When the Catholics in 1793 were not satisfied with his leave to them to vote for Protestant masters; when he saw that any conciliation that gave the Catholics too much would offend the Whig oligarchy, then he bent his mind to the union; and it was his money, his martial law, his bribery, his rebellion, his troops that forced it on. Pitt was cunning, always afraid of being overreached, and sure to sow distrust. He did so with Grattan and the volunteers in 1783; with Grattan and Fitzwilliam in 1795; with Catholics and Protestants in 1800. Pitt was insincere, unconstitutional, desperate, profligate, and violent; with flogging, strangling, and free quarters, by the pitch-cap, the triangle, the lash, and by an abominable set of agents, he governed Ireland and destroyed her unity with the empire.

[1] "Grattan's Life and Times," vol. v. p. 183.

Mr. Grattan urged the question of Catholic Emancipation on the occasion of his first speech in the Imperial Parliament, 1805, which Pitt applauded, and Byron describes, and when the majority against was 212. He urged it in his last speech in 1819, when the majority against was only two. It was not however till O'Connell's election for Clare, in 1828, that Peel and Wellington yielded to the Irish people, as in the following year they also abandoned the penal code. They then excluded O'Connell, who had been elected, and disfranchised the 40s. freeholders who had elected him.

But listen (it is worth while) to Peel's indictment of his master's policy:

"I ask you to examine the state of His Majesty's Government for the last thirty-five years. . . . I begin with 1794. From that period there has been disunion in the Government on account of the Catholic question, and the administration of Irish affairs. The consequences have been most unfavourable to the administration of the affairs of this country (England). The cabinets have been in general nearly equally divided. Ireland has been governed, almost inevitably, upon the same principle—at one time a Lord-Lieutenant adverse, and a Secretary favourable. The law offices of Ireland divided; the subordinate members also. What has been the consequence? Jealousies and suspicions between honourable men embarked in the same cause, and subject to the same responsibilities.

"Let us now turn to the legislature. . . . What is the result? Each party can paralyze the other; nothing effectual can be done, either by the means of coercion or relief. But what becomes of Ireland if these party conflicts without a result shall continue? I will not presume to affirm that the dissensions in our councils and the distractions of Ireland stand to each other in the exact relation of cause and effect, but they have been very nearly concurrent.

"Let us cast a rapid glance over the recent history of Ireland, trace it from the Union. What is the melancholy fact? That for scarcely one year during the period that has elapsed since the Union has Ireland been governed by the ordinary course of law.

"In 1800 we find the Habeas Corpus Act suspended, and the Act for the suppression of rebellion in force. In 1801 they were continued. In 1803 both Acts were renewed. In 1804 they were continued. In 1806 the west and south of Ireland were in a state of insubordination, which was with difficulty repressed by the severest enforcement of the ordinary law. In 1807 the Act called the 'Insurrection Act' was introduced. It gave power to the Lord-Lieutenant to place any district by proclamation out of the pale of the ordinary law; it suspended trial by jury, and made it a transportable offence to be out of doors from sunset to sunrise. In 1807 this Act continued in force, and in 1808-9, and to the close of the session of 1810. In 1814 the Insurrection Act was renewed: it was continued in 1815, '16, and '17. In 1822 it was again revived, and continued during the years 1823, '24, and '25. In 1825 the temporary Act intended for the suppression of dangerous associations was passed. It continued during 1826 and 1827, and expired in 1828. The year 1829 has arrived, and with it the demand for a new Act to suppress the Roman Catholic association."[1]

"Put down," exclaimed Lord Palmerston, "the Association! They might as well talk of putting down the winds of heaven, or of chaining the ceaseless tides of the ocean. . . . The Catholic Association was the people of Ireland. Its spirit was caused by the grievance of the nation; and its seat was the bosom of seven millions of its population. It was therefore idle to talk of putting down the Association except by removing the cause to which the Association owed its existence."[2]

It must be a prosperous country truly that needs yearly coercion Acts, and where it is a transportable offence to be out between sunset and sunrise!

But the desperate policy of Pitt became the desperate policy of Peel, who declared (1827) he would never alter it; but who (in 1829) found that a policy desperate for Ireland would speedily become desperate for himself, and then suddenly despaired of it and revoked it. But then he

[1] Mr. Secretary Peel, March 5, 1829. Hansard.
[2] February 10, 1829. Hansard.

had gone too far. The danger of Irish relenting was passed. O'Connell had roused the national spirit. The English conscience began to get informed, and emancipated Catholics and emancipated reforming Protestants in both countries were drawn together. Peel disfranchised Ireland, till O'Connell stopped him. He starved England till Cobden stopped him. When the bread of office could "no longer be leavened" with starvation and proscription, he preferred office; and when he tried to get away with the laurels of Free Trade, Disraeli stopped him, and stripped them from his brow.

"The Precursor Association declared," says O'Connell, "in the name and with the assent of the Irish people, that they might have consented to the continuance of the Union, if justice had been done them, if the franchise had been simplified and much extended, if the corporations had been reformed and continued, if the number of Irish members had been augmented in a just proportion, and if the tithe system had been abolished and conscience left completely free. But, on the other hand, these just claims being rejected. . . . the Irish people are too numerous, too wise, and too good to despair or to hesitate on the course they should adopt. The restoration of the national legislature is, therefore, again insisted on. . . . No honest man ever despaired of his country . . . Ireland will assert her rights for herself, preserving the golden and unonerous link of the Crown, true to the principles of unaffected and genuine allegiance, but determined, while she preserves her loyalty to the British throne, to vindicate her title to constitutional freedom for the Irish people." [1]

Peel prevented the danger of compromise, if it ever existed, and held on to obstructions, till O'Connell's great work was irrevocable and secure.

With the foreign and Irish policy of Pitt, with George III., never so much out of his senses as when he was in them, with the Irish not united, and the English not instructed, little was or could have been done at first, for

[1] Memoir, pp. 41, 42.

famine and injustice could not fail to officer and form the Irish army of agitation or vengeance. Even the Emancipation Act of 1828 contained "Church protection clauses for the suppression of the Catholic ecclesiastical orders," armed, at the instance of the Protestant Church Establishment party, with penalties of banishment and transportation; and the national bankruptcy of Ireland consequent on the Union; the futile Report, never acted on, of the great Devon Land Law Commission of 1845; the famines and the three insurrections; the vast increase of American-Irish, and the establishment of the first Irish national press—all have combined with English apathy, ignorance, and obstruction, and especially with the infatuation of the English House of Lords, to work up Ireland to that white heat of desperation of which James Fintan Lalor, in his organ, *The Irish Felon*, began to avail himself in 1848, and by which alone, according to our former way of ruling, great national reforms become possible.

Mr. Gladstone, in the debate on his Statutory Parliament Bill for Ireland, says that—

"Irish history on these matters in his time divided itself into three great periods. . . . The first was the Repeal period under Mr. O'Connell, which began about the time of the Reform Act, and lasted until the death of that distinguished man. The second period was that between the death of Mr. O'Connell, and the emergence of the subject of Home Rule. That was the period in which physical force and organization were conceived and matured, taking effect under the name generally of what is known as Fenianism. In 1870 or 1871 came up the question of Home Rule." [1]

The Premier's division can be followed as regards the O'Connell period, the direct ending being marked by his death, although influences that never die can hardly be

[1] May 10, 1886, *The Times* report.

said to have a period. But "the period of physical force and organization," and of preparation for Home Rule, are one, and, whatever we hope or fear, will last until the triumph of the principle of Irish nationality. The disintegration of English parties, the decomposition of imperial politics, and the confusion and postponement of the first fruits of confederation, will last exactly the same time.

The degradation of Protestant landlordism had been one of the results of earlier penal legislation, and the substitution of priests for landlords as leaders of the people was one of the direct consequences of Pitt's Catholic exclusion, and was organized and systematized by O'Connell, whose great Catholic association was formed in 1824, ramified the whole country, and was directed in every parish by the priest. At last, the whole mass of the people were organized like an army, and assembled in every part of the country on the same day. In 1828 it was conputed that in a single day two thousand meetings were held. O'Connell's object was to inspirit the people by a tone of unmeasured defiance and exaltation, and his Church entered into the conflict triumphant and unshackled—an object of fear not of contempt.

"Of all possible measures," says Lecky, "Catholic Emancipation might, if judiciously carried, have been most efficacious in making Ireland permanently loyal. The Irish Parliament governed chiefly by corruption, the landlords who controlled most of the votes were beyond all others exposed to temptation. They were also subject to the same demoralizing process as that which degrades the slave-owner. 'A landlord in Ireland,' said Arthur Young, 'can scarcely invent an order which a servant, labourer, or cottier dares refuse to execute.' The penal laws (which gave the whole estate of a Catholic to any son who abjured his religion) seemed ingeniously contrived to secure a perpetual influx of unprincipled men into the landlord class."

When at last reform, greatly helped by O'Connell, triumphed in 1832, the new parliament began by a stringent

Irish Coercion Bill. Secret societies ramified the country, the bonds of society were broken, law was discredited, and class warfare and religious animosity became supreme.

In 1833, the year in which O'Connell showed so noble and large-minded an example, by seconding the motion in the English House for the abolition of the Corn Laws, there was not in Ireland a single Catholic judge or stipendiary magistrate. The chief towns were in the hands of narrow and corrupt corporations. The Irish Secretary, Mr. Stanley, was intensely hated, and all tended to turn the people's minds to Repeal. The poorest Catholic cottager was compelled to pay something to support the hostile and aggressive Church of the rich minority. In one parish 222 tithe defaulters owed one farthing each, and a very large proportion throughout the country not more than 1s. each. At last a conspiracy to refuse payment spread over the land. Government advanced £60,000 in 1832, and undertook to collect the tithes of 1831, the arrears being £104,000. After much bloodshed it recovered £12,000, at a cost of £15,000; more than 9,000 crimes were perpetrated in Ireland in 1832 connected with the disturbed state of the country, and among them nearly 200 cases of homicide. It was at this time, says Mr. Lecky, that O'Connell talked of the "base, brutal, and bloody Whigs," men with "brains of lead, and hearts of stone, and fangs of iron." Lord Grey retired from office, and Lord Melbourne came in with O'Connell's support. The great subject then discussed was the Irish Church, and the Church Temporalities Act of 1833 made the Establishment more defensible, by which ten bishops and Church rates were abolished. O'Connell appears to have settled on a tithe plan, explained in a letter to Mr. Sharman Crawford in 1834, which was later adopted by Mr. Gladstone. The tithes composition measure of 1838 was also conceded to violence, and has not proved final, but has eradicated much crime and allayed a dangerous agitation.

In 1831-2 a system of national education was founded in Ireland, which continues, though seriously modified, to this day. It was intended to give the whole people a united secular education, while offering facilities for separate religious teaching. The liberal education policy of the Whigs was fully adopted, and extended by the Tories and Sir Robert Peel. In 1838 the Irish Poor Law was enacted. In 1835 Lord Melbourne brought in an Irish Corporation Bill, but the Lords wanted to abolish all Irish municipal government and to substitute State functionaries, and the Bill was not passed till 1840, when fifty-eight corporations were abolished. This Bill gave the inhabitants of towns the right to elect town councillors, and O'Connell was the first Catholic Mayor of Dublin, but the choice of the sheriff who had charge of the jury lists was in the hands of the Viceroy. All these measures were passed under the influence of the movement against Protestant ascendency.

"In agitating for Repeal, O'Connell," writes Mr. W. A. O'Conor,[1] "made his country potentially a nation. He gave it the power of rising to the voice of one man. He infused the spirit that keeps the pulses of Irishmen in all parts of the globe beating to one measure. He took the cause of independence out of the hands of a faction, and made it the life of the country."

"In the emancipation struggle, the Presbyterians of the North and the Reformers of England became O'Connell's natural allies. The intellects of England and Ireland found a common platform. O'Connell had always placed fixity of tenure among the first results of repeal of the Union, but the commission of landlords, appointed in 1844, condemned tenant right, and recommended consolidation of lands and emigration.

"A constitutionalist by nature, and shocked, in the dawn of his manhood, by the excesses of France where he was educated, O'Connell chose moral agitation for his country's deliverance. But his peaceful struggle was conducted with shout and onset of the

[1] "History of the Irish People," p. 280. Heywood, London, 1886.

warrior. He roused, united, and informed his countrymen. He inspired one soul into Ireland. He taught the people their power, and lifted them to a height of courage and consentaneous action from which they have never fallen. He made them one mass, inspired by one mind, and capable of following one chief. At the same time, he powerfully appealed to the reason and sympathy of Englishmen, and contributed to the growth of English liberties. The tyrants of both nations he dared and defied. His gait as he trod the streets was a challenge to those who demanded servile demeanour. We can scarcely now estimate his towering character, as he stood alone in the valley white with the skeletons of centuries, and prophesied upon them, and covered them with flesh and sinew and skin, and called the breath of freedom from the four winds to breathe upon them till they stood on their feet an exceeding great army. The magic of his sonorous voice, pealing over a desert, is lost to us who know of him only when his accents are drowned in the million echoes they have created. Emancipation was made not a sectarian question. O'Connell, with the mind and voice of the people, proclaimed a universal principle, and demanded for every religion absolute spiritual freedom."

"An association was formed at Birmingham on the exact model of the Catholic association in Dublin, and reform was won, O'Connell giving it every assistance in his power. Thus we find O'Connell at one and the same time contending with England when she opposed justice in Ireland, and co-operating with her, heart and soul, when she struggled for the deliverance of her own people, and for human rights in any part of the globe."

When Walter Savage Landor addressed a petition to the Queen for a free pardon for O'Connell and the other Irish State prisoners, the reasons he adduced were as follows:

"The act of union was brought about by practices which would disfranchise any borough in England; because Ireland at the present moment was treated with less liberty in regard to religion than Greece under the dominion of the Turks; because two millions of British subjects in America, who had incomparably less cause of complaint than Ireland, were driven to sever themselves from the dominion of England, whereas Ireland contained seven millions, and the nearest and most powerful nations sympathized with her cause; because O'Connell had alone restrained the passions of his countrymen, and had maintained a state of tranquillity which no other man for six hundred years had been able to establish."

"In no instance," says Lecky, "did O'Connell's meetings degenerate into mobs. He worked with Father Mathew, and considered the teetotalers as his policemen. He had no rival. He transformed the whole social system of Ireland; almost reversed the relative positions of Protestants and Roman Catholics; remodelled by his influence the representative, ecclesiastical, educational institutions; created the elements of his own power, governed the people absolutely and long, made the Liberal party in Ireland synonymous with the Catholic party, and created a public opinion that surpassed the wildest dreams of his predecessors. He anticipated very accurately the Bill which has recently passed, saying, 'Nothing will do but giving some kind of fixity of tenure to the occupier, and especially an absolute right of recompense for all substantial improvements.'" [1]

"The great contrast between O'Connell's influence now culminating and that of 'Young Ireland' was that he was supposed not to be prepared to countenance bloodshed. He prepared, however, for the coming of 'Young Ireland' by his lifelong attempts to break or weaken the landed classes, and by making priests the political leaders of the people. If, at the present moment, the antagonism of classes and creeds is stronger in Ireland than in any other country in Europe, this is to be mainly attributed to the policy of Pitt, and to the agitation of O'Connell." [2]

The "Young Irelanders" were chiefly Protestants, were more independent of priests, sympathized rather with 1798 than 1782, and were prepared to stand either without the law or within it.

Sir Charles Gavan Duffy thus introduces O'Connell's summary, given in 1843, of the injuries of the Union, which must be noted here:

[1] Lecky, pp. 297-9, 1871 edition.   [2] Lecky on O'Connell, p. 310.

"Every one knew that the ancient seat of industry in the liberties was now a pauper-warren, that the stately edifices erected by an Irish parliament for international commerce were the offices of tax-gatherers, that the palaces of the resident nobility had become museums and mendicities, and the Woollen Hall, from which the produce of five thousand looms was once circulated, a poor-house crowded with weavers without work."[1]

And then he quotes O'Connell:

"The Union was a profitable compact for one of the parties. England found a market for her fabrics, a recruiting field for her army, a partner in her public burthens, and by making absenteeism a necessity for members of parliament and their train, she drew from Ireland an annual tribute of five or six millions rent.

"But for the other partner it was a disastrous compact. Before the Union Ireland was the seat of flourishing woollen and silk manufactories. The woollen trade had taken root prior to the revolution of 1688, but on the demand of the English Parliament, though in the hands of Protestants, it nearly disappeared. A hundred years later, when Grattan had established legislative independence, the trade sprang up under the care of a free parliament, and at the period of the Union the cloth loom was at work in Dublin, Kilkenny, Limerick, Carrick-on-Suir, Roscrea, and several smaller towns. The population of Ireland was then only four millions, of whom one hundred and fifty thousand were employed in silk and woollen manufactures. In 1841 the population had increased to eight and nine millions, but the number of these artizans had shrunk to a handful—fewer than eight thousand. The mills in the provincial towns were all closed; in Dublin, where ninety master manufacturers had given employment to five thousand artisans, the former had diminished to twelve, and the latter to less than seven hundred. The fate of the remainder might be learned from the mendicity society."

"At the commencement of the French war the Irish National Debt was two millions and a quarter, that of England two hundred and forty millions. An Irish debt was created in her name

[1] "Young Ireland," p. 29. Cassell.

during the war by undue military expenditure, by a pension list on which English courtezans and favourites, spies and jobbers, were silently quartered by Royal authority, and by the trick of charging as Irish national expenditure the money employed by English statesmen to purchase votes in favour of the Union. She suffered the fate of men and nations who entrust their interests to strangers.

"To protect and continue this system it was necessary to diminish the political power of Ireland, and Parliament was deliberately packed. Scotland, by the Reform Act, got an increase of one to five of her existing representatives, Wales one to six, Ireland one to twenty. In 1834 Irish corporations were exclusively in the hands of Protestants, and were reeking with corruption. Ireland was contemptuously refused corporate reform. The union had ruined merchants, traders, and artisans; and the peasantry fared no better. The Poor Law Commissioners computed the number of agricultural labourers to be over a million, and ascertained that one-half of these were out of employment for thirty weeks in the year."

And Sir C. Gavan Duffy adds:

"Harbours looking towards the prosperous Western world were completely vacant; harbours looking toward the East were occupied only by ships which carried raw produce and food to England. There was no foreign trade: the wines of Spain and Portugal, the silks of France, the drugs and spices of the East, the timber of the North only reached the island through England. The noble quays of the Liffey, which would rival the Lung d'Arno of Florence, were the seat of a national government, and held only a few canal barges and fruit boats. There was scarcely a county which could not show some public work begun before the union, and now a ruin.

"The great proprietors were two or three hundred, the mass of the country was owned by two or three thousand others, who lived in splendour. Rent meant the whole of the produce except a potato pit. If the farmer strove for more his master could carry away his implements of trade, and habitually seized the stools and pots in the cabin, the blanket that sheltered the children, the cow that gave them nourishment. The mild Berkeley spoke of Irish proprietors as vultures with iron bowels."[1]

"The Irish landlords made a law that when the tenant planted a tree it became his master's property; and the established practice of four-fifths of the Irish landlords, when the tenant established such property as a garden or a whitewashed cottage, was to raise his rent."

And referring to O'Connell's difficult position, Mr. John Morley lately thus retorted on a "Unionist" debater:

"Where you had in O'Connell's time a constituency of 150,000, and a population of 8,000,000, you have now nearly 750,000 voters in a population of less than 5,000,000. O'Connell died in 1847. That was the era of the famine. The famine was followed by the great emigration and the wholesale eviction—a chapter of which we have not yet come to the last page. That was a dismemberment and a dispersion which planted in every quarter of the globe an enemy to your rule. That is the most important of all the changes, because the growth of an Ireland across the seas has given the Irish at home a self-confidence and a moral power, and a command of material resources of which O'Connell never dreamed."[2]

There were but three possible ways in which O'Connell, or any one else, could contend with England. The first was the Parliamentary franchise, but the Irish voters were simply outnumbered and lost in the multitude of their opponents; besides which, on O'Connell's election, Peel and Wellington at once disfranchised the 40s. freeholders who had returned him. The second would have been a great soldier with an armed nucleus, but Pitt and Wellington had crammed 35,000 soldiers into Ireland, and ships of war were all round the coast.[3] The third method would have been that now used by Mr. Parnell—the Parliamentary followers; but O'Connell had only the 26. Moreover, in his time, the native press had not much

---

[1] See "Young Ireland," pp. 139-140, and 142.
[2] *Times* report, June 4, 1886.
[3] See "The Parnell Movement."

ability, and when a really able paper appeared, it advocated more direct and drastic measures than his.

Now, taking the Irish census for the decades 1821-31-41, we find the population increase from 6,800,000 to 7,700,000 and 8,100,000; and in the three and a half months in 1841, from May 13th to August 31st, 57,651 persons migrated from Ireland to Great Britain (presumably for work in the hay and corn harvest), whilst during the latter decade (ending 6th of June, 1841) 214,647 went from home (most of them, namely, 189,225, to British America), and only 19,775 to the United States. But before 1851 everything seems changed. From 1845 to 1868, three millions would probably not be an over-estimate of Irish emigration to the United States, and the census shows the population gone back to 6,500,000—actually below that of 1821 (and 1,600,000 less than that of 1841).

Here, then, were the bases for agitation. The landlord class continued to deny their duties with a brow of brass, and to exact their rights with a hand of iron. The potato famine of 1846-7-8 was followed by the insurrection of 1848, and emigration increased in numbers, and was diverted from British America to the United States. Five years also had elapsed since the Devon Commission began to sit, three since it had reported, and none of the recommendations had been acted on.

The Protestant Church established and the Whig Protestant landowning junto were yet too strong; nor had the Irish found their fulcrum.

"When O'Connell had made up his mind to raise the repeal cry once more, he sent for Mr. Ray, and told him, 'I sent for you, Ray, to tell you I have done experimenting on the British Parliament. I shall now go for repeal.' But he still postponed this till Easter, 1840, and did not establish his new association until Lord Stanley had outraged the people of Ireland by his Bill to still further diminish their restricted franchise." [1]

[1] Daunt's "Personal Recollections of O'Connell," vol. i. p. 59.

In 1843 came the year of O'Connell's monster meetings, Sir R. Peel having declared that there was "no influence, power, or authority, which the prerogative of the Crown and existing laws gave the Government, which should not be exercised for the purpose of maintaining the union." The organization of the repealers was almost perfect, and reached its full dimensions. The rents were collected through the clergy, and repeal wardens, under O'Connell, managed the district. Usually these vast meetings were held on Sunday upon the hillside, the mighty throng kneeling on the green-sward around their priests with their hundred altars. O'Connell had almost reversed the relative positions of Catholics and Protestants. This achievement is best described by his own grand book: "Grattan sat by the cradle of his country, and followed her hearse; it was left for me to sound the resurrection trumpet, and to show that she was not dead, but sleeping."

Any who fancy that the present movement is ephemeral, or not national, should read Sir Charles Gavan Duffy's account from notes written shortly after, of "The Muster of the Nation at Tara," in 1843; and the letters written more than a generation since, in *The Morning Chronicle*, by Sir Charles Trevelyan, who, trained to vigilance amongst a dangerous population in India, went to Ireland regarding repeal as a gigantic piece of blarney, but found intense desire and genuine belief—found a people singularly sober, advancing in industry, good order, and respect for the laws. Though O'Connell might mean peace, the people meant fighting. At that time, moreover, a number of Presbyterian and Congregational clergymen, constantly travelling as missionaries in Munster and Connaught, declared that no sectarian passions were at work, and a few years later, Presbyterian ministers went as political missionaries to the South, and Catholic priests and the remnant of young Irelanders to the North, for the promotion of a common purpose—a secure tenure for the tenant farmers.

"At nine in the morning," writes Sir C. Gavan Duffy (greatly compressed by me), "a small train of private carriages, containing O'Connell and a few friends, set out from Merrion Square. Carriages containing members of the Corporation in their robes of office, and other notable citizens, fell silently in at various points, and in the suburbs a long line of jaunting cars, and the *cortége* became a procession. Through a succession of villages, hamlets, and towns the entire population was afoot in holiday dress, and the houses were decorated with banners on evergreens. Each local muster, headed by its local band, took its place. At three toll gates 1,300 vehicles paid toll, and 10,000 horsemen attended O'Connell. A dozen miles from the historic hill large crowds were met with, who had come from distant places during the night and bivouacked in the green pastures of Meath under the August sky. A little later, the repealers of Kells, Trim, and Navan joined, each town preceded by its band in the national uniform of green and white, and by banners, mustered by mounted marshals, horsemen four deep, footmen six deep, marching as in battalions. Three miles from the hill the vehicles had to be left. Around the base the bands and banners were mustered—the bands forty, the banners past counting.

"The procession, however, was but as a river discharging itself into the ocean. The whole district was covered with men. The population within a day's march began to arrive shortly before daybreak, and continued to arrive, on all sides by every available approach, till noon. It was impossible from any one point to see the entire meeting. Hill and plain were covered with a multitude countless as the bearded grain. Such a muster never before assembled in one place in Ireland, and they met and parted without offence, altercation, or accident. Three-fourths were probably teetotalers, kept in discipline not only by cool brains, but by pride of class. Three loiterers, twenty miles from the hill, admitted that the teetotalers of the parish would not let them march because they had broken the pledge. Women probably formed a fifth, and their presence was a further restraint. At least, all knew that there on the hill stood the council palace of Irish princes; that there St. Patrick had preached, and men of Irish birth fought for national independence.

"Before O'Connell's arrival successive troops visited the 'Mound of the hostages,' the 'Stone of destiny,' and the site of Temara, but the deepest enthusiasm was reserved for the 'Croppie's grave.' Twenty banners were planted around it, and the people knelt down bareheaded, praying for the souls that had died for Ireland. On his arrival the bands saluted O'Connell with triumphant music, and blessed him who typified their desire to be once again a nation. . . .

"There were more men present than possessed Scotland when Wallace raised the standard of independence, or Athens in the days of her world renown. They were possessed by the intense conviction that made irresistible soldiers of farmers and farm labourers under Cromwell and Washington, and a new nation might have been born that day.

"Peel would not fight (said clubs and *quidnuncs*). Thirty meetings had (on Sunday, October 5, 1843, the day for the Clontarf meeting) been held. The nation so long without a senate, a flag, an army, a judiciary, or a Government, had recreated a national organism with the rudiments of all these institutions. A virtual Government sat in Conciliation Hall; a popular and trusted magistracy had begun to administer justice in the Arbitration Courts; a fund equivalent to a poll tax was regularly paid by voluntary contributions; and an army in numbers, obedience, and almost in discipline, gathered round the green flag wherever it was hoisted. The executive of the United States had at its head an avowed repealer. Foreign nations tendered that passive and active sympathy which is so formidable, and which enabled the Netherlands in the seventeenth century, and the North American Colonies in the eighteenth, and Greece and Belgium in the nineteenth to triumph.

"In 1843 the occasion for a stand in defence had come if it ever could come. The two main conditions existed—there were intolerable wrongs for which a peaceful remedy was scornfully refused, and there were solid grounds for expecting success. A nation of eight millions fighting to keep their country is an immense force. Nine-tenths of the men capable of bearing arms were repealers, and flushed with the passionate belief that theirs was the wonder-working cause of Divine and human justice.

"But on Saturday, at noon, the committee of the association met at the Corn Exchange to await the threatened proclamation and prohibition. Government made no sign other than the arrival of five fresh regiments from England and Scotland. The grey of evening came, and at half-past three the proclamation. In two hours it could not be read. At dawn the masses would move, and already repealers had come from Manchester, Liverpool, and Belfast, and other places remote."[1]

O'Connell's proclamation to submit was posted within twenty miles of Clontarf during the night, and at dawn his agents and the Catholic clergy explained and enforced it. When day dawned, Conquer Hill, a site overlooking the ancient battle-field, was occupied by horse, foot, and artillery, the latter unlimbered and with lighted matches.

The cause was lost for that time. To have brought the repealers to this pass was described as a masterstroke of Peel's.

"As for Wellington, we learn from Raike's diary," says Sir Charles Gavan Duffy, "that he muttered several times, as he went into dinner, much elated at the news:

> Pour la canaille
> Faut la mitraille.

"The barracks were pierced with loopholes, and became fortresses against insurrection. Forts and martello towers were put in a state of defence. Garrisons were strengthened, the supply of arms and materiel of war were largely increased, and war steamers were stationed on the sea coast and navigable rivers. The soldiers who attended Catholic churches went in marching order, with guns, bayonets, and knapsacks ready for immediate service."

As to O'Connell, his mighty soul racked with agony, and possibly at this point commencing to suffer from that brain softening of which he died, he exclaimed to the one or two intimates with whom he dared unbend, "My God, my God, what shall I do with this people!"

[1] Pp. 344-7.

In his duel with Peel, O'Connell won the nation's soul, and lost for a while its body, which was delivered over to the two tormentors—Irish landlords and an English Parliament ignorant of Ireland—for another of Lord Salisbury's epochs.

Things went on to the next stage, according to the logic of events "and weapons." The British Cabinet swept the field clear of moral influence, and have seemed considerably surprised ever since at something else taking it.

On October 12, 1842, appeared the first number of *The Nation*, Mr. C. Gavan Duffy being the proprietor, and John Mitchell and John Dillon amongst its writers. A tremendous power was exercised by the first national press, now managed with conspicuous ability. Events were getting far beyond O'Connell's influence, and John Mitchell's *United Irishman*, and later on John Martin's *Irish Felon*, became the Irish American classics. Their ultimate aim was Home Rule; their immediate means, an Irish party in the English House, and not reliance on an English party.

The last clause of the prospectus of *The Nation* is worth remembering :

"Nationality is the projectors' first great object—a nationality which will not only raise our people from their poverty by securing to them the blessings of a DOMESTIC LEGISLATION, but inflame and purify them with a lofty and heroic love of country—a nationality of the spirit as well as the letter—a nationality which may come to be stamped upon our manners, our literature, and our deeds—a nationality which may embrace Protestant, Catholic, and Dissenter, Milesian and Cromwellian—the Irishman of a hundred generations, and the stranger who is within our gates; not a nationality which would prelude civil war, but which would establish internal union and external independence—a nationality which would be recognized by the world, and sanctioned by wisdom, virtue, and prudence."

And also the teaching of *The Nation*:

"Every law which produced on the whole more misery than happiness was wicked, and ought to be abolished or resisted. But resistance often meant death by cold and hunger. It was time to inquire why should landowners in Ireland be the only class of creditors possessing the power of life and death.

"To win and sustain her rank as a nation, Ireland must possess the elements that constitute a nation in a high degree. In position, climate, coasts, and soil, she had them in the highest, and in population and wealth sufficiently high. But she wanted an ample supply of public men, and she wanted literature and art.

"When a people have the boundaries of history, the separate character, and physical resources, and still more, the virtue and genius of a nation, they are bound in conscience, in prudence, and in wisdom to attest their individuality, no matter how conciliation may lure or armies threaten."

In 1845 we come to the report of the famous Devon Commission. It sat for two years, examined over 1110 witnesses, visited every county in Ireland and ninety-six towns, was embodied in fourteen volumes, and might as well, for all the English cared or knew, have been buried in an Irish bog or in bottomless Hades. It recommended certain precise and practicable remedies, declared the evidence "conclusive, pressing, and portentous," and that the safety of the country called for immediate adjustment of interests. This commission thus examined, concluded, recommenced, and vanished into space more than a generation ago, and it is time for another to sit and vanish. Nothing came of it; but a good deal came of that nothing. It was duly succeeded by famine, desolation, evictions, assassination, war—but all these were Irish. It was not till Englishmen of eminence and rank were murdered that England woke up to the fact that "something must be done."

Daniel O'Connell, M.P., was examined on January 28, 1845. He was the 1110th witness; his evidence appears in the report under that number, and it relates back to the Union, the objects and intention of that Union, and onwards to its consequences. He said :

"There are two prominent causes of distress in Ireland : first, insecurity of tenure; second, the enormous power of working out his will which the landlord has by statute law—a power which has increased exceedingly since 1800. The landlord is all-powerful, and as to legal redress, even against a plainly unlawful act, there is none, I may say, for the peasant. An attorney would cost more than he has got together during his life; and then, as laid down by Chief Justice Pennefather, the law contemplates the interests of the landlord alone.

"The supply of land is not equal to the demand. The tenant is obliged to take the land at any price. If things go on as they do, murders will accumulate, and fixity of tenure will be conquered from the landlords by fear. It was a phrase of Lord Clare's that 'a landlord of straw could grind a tenant of steel,' and since his time the power of the landlords has been very much increased. There was, before 1800, no power to eject tenants except through expensive process in superior courts, costing £18 to £150. That operated as a caution to be more select in their tenants. [It also must have given comparative fixity of tenure.] But now for a few shillings a tenant can be ejected, and there is no sacredness of possession."

According to other evidence on this head, an occupying tenant could be ejected or distrained on by the paramount landlord for rent already paid to the immediate landlord; and notice of process had been reduced from thirty days to fifteen.

"And," continued O'Connell, "then there are the stamp duties, and a man is legally, but unjustly evicted. I know a district where not one tenant has a valid lease because of the want of the stamp. The horrible massacre of the Sheas in Tipperary was thus occasioned. An entire family were surrounded in their house, and most were burnt to death; such as attempted to escape were slaughtered outside.

"It is since 1800 that power of selling and distraining growing crops was given in Ireland.

"I don't think there is anything in nature by which greater oppression can be practised. The growing crop seized generally consists of the daily food of the peasant. It is seized in the month of September, for example. Before the seizure he digs a certain portion for his daily meal; by seizure nothing is left for him to subsist on. If he digs, it is 'rescuing a distress,' or wilful trespass, and he is sent to gaol and his family left to starve.

"Another great cause is the Wilful Trespass Act, which gives a frightful dominion to the landlord class. In truth, it has annihilated all the smaller rights of passage, turf-cutting, sea-weed cutting below low water mark; also the right of drawing sand and using footways of long standing. This is one of the maddening stimulants to crime."

What, then, did this commission find, and what did it recommend?

It found that there had been thirteen committees and reports before its own, and not one acted on; that one-fourth or one-fifth of the population was out of employment, and badly housed, clad, fed, and paid; it found the great and enduring patience of the people; it found a total area in acres of 20,808,271, of which there were 6,295,735, or nearly one-third, uncultivated, and 1,486,764 only, or one-fourteenth of the whole, absolutely useless by nature.

It found no arterial drainage, and no quays or roads; superfluous fish, but no fishing piers.

It found 65,000 tillage farms under one acre; 600,000 farmers, and that 500,000 of them were tenants-at-will.

It found that it was not the custom for the landlord to build dwelling-houses, or farm offices, or to make drains, fences, or gates; that the peasant's usual house was one room, and that the usual family included cow and pigs; that potatoes were often the only food, water the only drink; that the cabin let in wet, that bed and blanket were rare luxuries; that any advantage the peasant wrested from fate was due almost entirely to temperance.

It found by evidence abundant, overwhelming, portentous, that the safety of the country demanded an immediate adjustment of landlord and tenant rights.

It found that with high coast lines, vast interior plains, humid climate, all Ireland except the rocks, was one vast sponge,—the soil cold, and even the sun going wrong, because it has to evaporate moisture instead of ripening crops.

It found methodized war all over Ireland for the Ulster tenant-right. A tenant-right was prevalent in the three southern provinces, but the price paid by the incomer was not large, and consequently the landlord could not select his tenant as in Ulster, nor could either party be so secure.

It found—for in Appendix No. 89 it quotes the census of 1841—that there were four classes of house accommodation; the fourth being mud cabins with only one room; the third, mud cabins with from two to four rooms: and in the 32 counties of Ireland, over 42 per cent., or nearly one-half of the population, occupied the fourth class, that is to say, mud cabins with only one room, and 80 per cent., or nearly the entire labouring population, dwelt in the third or fourth class.

The Devon Commission recommended a good many things, but chiefly and simply: (1) the registration of agreements as to improvement, and, in default of such registration, (2) power to ascertain and certify the maximum cost and value of them not exceeding three years' rent; and (3) valuation in case of ejectment.

The English Government took no action on the Devon Commission, and soon the famine was upon them.

With the famine came the occasion which showed what was the Union, and where were the real representatives of

Ireland. The Corporation of Dublin implored an early meeting of parliament, and the use of public money in public works. The Duke of Leinster, the Lord Mayor, O'Connell, and others, waited on the Viceroy and recommended the opening of the ports to foreign corn, the stoppage of the distillation from grain, &c. Their advice Peel did not take.[1]

Later on, the "Young Irelanders," led by O'Brien, formed themselves into the Irish confederation, and separated from O'Connell, their avowed object being armed insurrection, and not moral force.

If we look at the dates of English administrations at this time, we shall see that Peel and our own Corn Laws were in in 1841, Earl Russell in 1846, Lord Derby in 1852, and the Earl of Aberdeen also, and that Palmerston came in in 1855. All these statesmen had things more important than our home empire to attend to. Their eyes were on the ends of the earth, with the result mentioned by Solomon in the Book of Proverbs. They were bolstering up Turkish and Austrian tyranny; betraying Hungary; bullying China into buying Indian opium; keeping back the penny newspapers, whose promoters said, "Let us have light;" and turning out Cobden and Bright, who said, "Let us have peace and non-intervention abroad, and vigilance and freedom at home." For these good reasons they neglected real English and Irish questions: to needy English tax-paying knife-grinders who wanted abatements, they made Canning's reply; and to Irish appeals for bread, they offered "Devon" stones.

The value of the Devon Commission was, not that it recommended anything extraordinary, but that having probed the Irish mischief simply and profoundly, its suggestions were adequate, had they been acted on then, to stay the plague of famine, desolation, and war, that has since paralyzed England, and outraged the moral sense of

[1] "The Parnell Movement," p. 281.

the world. As it was, the famine came, and conquered and altered all things.

"Under the Soup Kitchen Relief Act," said the Hon. Gavan Duffy, in July, 1847, " 3,020,712 persons received separate rations in one day. The famine swallowed things more precious than money or lives—the temperance reformation, the political training of a generation, the self-respect, the purity and generosity which distinguished Irish Protestants. New and terrible diseases sprung up, and children were growing idiots. In eight of the worst unions, the contract coffin left the workhouse seventy times a week. There were two thousand cases of ophthalmia within ten months in the Tipperary Union, and as many in the Limerick one. In Connaught the famine created a new race with only a distant and hideous resemblance to humanity, and a traffic of wild, idle, lunatic-looking paupers—women struggling and screaming for coin like monstrous and unclean animals. I saw these accursed sights, and they are burned into my memory for ever. Poor mutilated, debased scions of a tender, brave, and pious stock; martyrs in the battle of centuries for the right to live in their own land." [1]

I here take two stories of evictions, the first in September, 1847, the same year as the famine, near Mount Nugent, Co. Cavan :

"Seven hundred human beings were driven from their homes on this one day. There was not a shilling of rent due on the estate at the time, except by one man. The sheriff's assistants employed to extinguish the hearths and demolish the homes of those honest industrious men stopped suddenly, and recoiled from two dwellings where was typhus fever. The agent insisted that these houses should come down, but ordered a large winnowing-sheet to be secured over the beds of the delirious fever victims, and then directed the houses to be unroofed cautiously and slowly. I administered the last sacraments to four of the victims next day, and save the winnowing-sheet, there was not then a roof nearer than the canopy of heaven. The

[1] See " The Parnell Movement," p. 122.

wailing of the women, the screams of the children, the agony of the men, wrung tears from all. I saw the officers and men of a large police force who were obliged to attend on the occasion cry like children. The heavy rains descended in torrents through the night. . . . I visited them next morning, and rode from place to place. The landed proprietors in a circle all round, and for many miles in all directions, warned the tenantry against admitting these poor people to even a single night's shelter. Many at last graduated from the workhouse to the tomb, and in little more than three years nearly a fourth of them lay quietly in their graves." [1]

It is useless to allege that these are rare occurrences. Unjust evictions are the natural history of Ireland. Even Sir Robert Peel was appalled at them, and said so in the House at the time of the Clare extermination:

"I must say I do not think the records of any country, civilized or barbarous, ever presented such a statement as that presented to the House in a letter by Captain Kennedy. This gentleman, an officer I believe in Her Majesty's Service, states that in one union—at a time of famine within one year, 15,000 persons have been driven from their homes; and that within the last month 1,200 more persons have had their houses levelled to the ground."

The second specimen I shall give is a narrative by Ellis Carr:[2]

"Under the rain stood a group of stalwart peasants, fiercely excited. Emerging from the road was a long double file of constabulary with fixed bayonets. On they came, two by two, gradually forming a half-circle round the cottages. Execrations rent the air; but a single look from the priest, and 'remember your promise, boys,' calmed the tumult.

"Already the women had come out of the cottages, and their sons and husbands had commenced to remove the household goods. But seated on a low chair, at the side of the empty hearth, was a very old man, and when the first piece of furniture was taken

[1] Summarised from the narrative of Dr. Nulty, Bishop of Meath (see "New Ireland," vol. i.). [2] Gill, Dublin.

out a change came over him, and he sat crying, wringing his hands, and rocking himself to and fro. First came the old camp bedstead, in which he and every child of his had smiled and wept in infancy, then the faded patchwork quilt, and the dresser his wife used to boast of. Then the spinning-wheel, on which the old man gazed, and in fancy saw half a century back his young bride at work, and he listening to her song as she kept time to the humming of the wheel. As his grief grew greater his granddaughter bent over him, and twining her arms round his neck like a mother soothing a child, stroked his aged head which rested on her breast. In a few minutes the old man was seen at the door leaning on the priest's arm, another moment and all would be over, but on the door-step he flung himself with a faint cry on his knees, clinging to the door-post, and pressing his lips again and again to the hard wood in despair and agony. In vain Molly used every endearment to coax him away. In vain the priest, who saw that the crowd would soon be beyond his control, spoke of the sorrows of Him who had not whereon to lay His head, and gently threw his arms round the old man to make him yield. Mat's lips moved convulsively, but no speech came from them. Then he gasped heavily, and with a deep sigh fell back dead."

One cannot help asking whose property was that doorpost and that cottage, and the cottages in the preceding story? According to the usual custom, the tenant reared those cottages, and paid rack-rent for that land. We have only to turn to Arthur Young's account of the reclamation by Whiteboys of an Irish mountain under a liberal landlord, to see and feel how loyal and good are the Irish with fair treatment; and we have only to imagine Sir William Osborne's successors to be rack-rented, to trace the inevitable results in outrage and reaction:

"Sir William Osborne owned a mountain in Waterford. The tenant thought it useless, and offered it him back without deduction of rent. Sir William met a beggar with a wife and six children in rags, built a cabin for him, gave him five acres and as much lime as he would come for. The man flourished, repaid the £4, and soon got twelve acres under cultivation, and in twelve years stock worth £80. Others applied, and Sir William fixed them on the same mountain, with terms ending with the lease of the farm; and they kept coming, though when Young visited the place only two years had to run. Thus Sir William has fixed twenty-two families, the meanest growing rich, and their industry has no bounds, nor is the day long enough for their incessant labour. He has told them that at the end of the lease a rent will be charged, and some have marked out thirty or forty acres which they wish to have on those terms. Nine-tenths of them were Whiteboys. In time they will take the whole mountain of nine hundred acres. The children work, and the women spin. The villainy of the greatest miscreants is all situation and circumstance. Give them property and the fruit of their labour. This Sir W. Osborne has done with the refuse of the Whiteboys. Yet in spite of such facts do the lazy, trifling, negligent, slobbering owners of Irish mountains leave them to the grouse and foxes."[1]

Mr. Wilfrid Blunt occupies a whole page in *The Pall Mall Gazette* of April 5, 1886, in telling the story of a similar mountain rack-rented, and how a landlord distrained and evicted his tenant because he owed his tenant £98 17s. 3d. His accuracy has been questioned, but condensing a good deal, and using Mr. Blunt's own words, this is how he says the trick is done:

"Just men would be shocked to find how the case runs between the Celtic peasant and the English peer. Some fourteen miles from Boyle is a tract of mountain land, and the little whitewashed houses of the tenants dot the landscape close to each other right up to the crest of the hills in plots of five to ten acres. The Celtic population, driven from the fatter lands of the plains, have reclaimed the soil at their own cost, and built these dwellings with their own hands. Although evictions had taken place after the famine, and the better lands been assumed by the landlords [this seems to have been universally the case in the famine time], the hill-tenants had not been very badly treated till recent years. The peculiarity of the Celtic peasantry, and what puts

[1] Arthur Young, "Mountain Improvements in Waterford by Whiteboys, 1787," pp. 326–8.

them at the mercy of their landlords, is that they submit to almost any injustice rather than be driven away. Land acquires, for an unscrupulous landlord, many times its commercial value, and the peasant may be despoiled over and over again before he will quit his holding. The agent not only raised all the rents, but in many cases decreased the acreage. The figures of a greater number shows increase of 50 per cent., double and sometimes nearly three times the old rent. The fancy demands of the landlords were met out of earnings in England, or pious offerings of relations who had crossed the Atlantic. The Land Act of 1881 seems to have brought little relief. The few who could afford to apply got their rent lowered. Now they are being evicted for a year or only half a year's rent.

"Drained by rack-rent, they have nothing to fall back upon. The price of stock has fallen, and the cost of rearing increased; yet on this Kilrouan estate I cannot discover that till last autumn the huge rents were greatly, or indeed at all, in arrears. In many instances, only the last half year. Father Reddy assures me that, except in one instance, he is absolutely certain that poverty alone is the cause of the present non-payment.

"Father Reddy, finding last autumn the tenants could not pay the whole rent, made an appeal for reductions; the tenants waited on the agent, and were served with writs at a cost of £1. Twelve tenants have been evicted a month ago, in the midst of the severe weather, with the aid of 180 constabulary, and three constables to each house are now guarding the 'emergency men' or caretakers. Next week fifty-three more households are threatened.

"I will now give you the commercial case between Pat McMann and the Earl of Kingston.

"Pat McMann is a little old man of seventy, much bent and bowed, but cheerful, born in 'the house yonder, where the soldiers are.' I found him in a neighbour's house. His house had been built by his father, who had originally taken five acres. Thirty years ago, he himself reclaimed two and a half acres more from the mountain, going to the valley for the lime and carrying it up in baskets on his head at a shilling the basket. He had paid £20 for the tenant right of another bit of eight acres, which the very next year the landlord had taken away without any compensation whatever. He paid £5 rent all but 2d. for the seven and a half acres. People advised him to go to the court, but where was he to get the money? In the autumn he was sued for rent £2 9s. 11d. and £1 fine, and now £3 12s. 10d. cost of eviction. He and his father had paid rent for seventy years. He believed, like Job, in the justice of God, and that he would get back one day before he died into his own house. The fields were of the poorest sort, the house built with his own father's hands, solid and weather-tight. His bed was occupied by the 'emergency man' and the three constables, who were cooking the old owner's potatoes.

	£	s.	d.
Pat owes Landlord	2	9	11
Costs	3	12	10
	6	2	9
Per Contra.			
A house	70	0	0
Two and a half acres reclaimed	10	0	0
Eight acres resumed without compensation	20	0	0
Fines	5	0	0
	105	0	0

"Balance of Pat's loss £98 17s. 3d.—that is to say, Pat, after seventy years' honest labour, is to die in the workhouse because the landlord owes him £98 17s. 3d."

This reminds one of Swift's recommendation to a parson whose church was dilapidated, to "give it to the Papists, and when they had repaired it to take it back," and which was much improved on by the landlord, who used at one time to hire naked land to the Papists, and when they had put it in working order took it back at his discretion.

In 1850 the Irish Tenant League was formed, Duffy and Frederick Lucas its chief journalists. In 1852, Lucas wrote of the Irish peasantry: "There is not in the world a people for whom a man of any heart or conscience would sooner lay down his life."

Fifty tenant-right members were now returned to parliament, pledged to oppose all Governments that did not allow the principle of tenant-right for all Ireland.

Between 1845 and 1885 emigration and hunger reduced the population one-half, and the half left was the worse. Seventy-five per cent. of the emigrants were between fifteen and thirty-five years of age. During seven months of 1863, wrote *The Times*, 80,000 young men and women left Ireland with money in their pockets, and strong limbs and stout hearts. They left behind them the ailing, the weak, and the aged.

> "This island," wrote *The Nation*, "is being quietly cleared—with its sixteen harbours, fertile soil, noble rivers, and beautiful lakes, fertile mines, and riches of every kind—is being quietly cleared for the interests and luxuries of humanity."[1]

Nemesis, however, was at hand, and from 1855 to 1865, and especially after the funeral of McManus in 1861, an active policy became more apparent. The civil wars in America had brought many thousands of exiled Irish into actual warfare, and made them familiar with the idea of liberating Ireland by arms. McManus was one of the 1848 leaders, and died at San Francisco in 1861. It was resolved to bury him in Ireland, and after a conflict with Archbishop Cullen and other authorities, a demonstration of 50,000 followed the remains, and at least as many lined the streets. The procession paused solemnly, with uncovered heads, at every spot sacred to Ireland, slackening in silent and stern defiance opposite the Castle. From this time the advance of Fenianism was rapid.[2]

Organizers went all over Ireland swearing in men by dozens or scores every night. It often happened that

[1] August 26, 1865.
[2] "The Parnell Movement," p. 208.

regiments passing through country towns cheered loudly in open air for the Irish Republic. By 1865 they had enrolled 15,000 men in the British army alone.

On June 24, 1848 (six years after *The Nation*), appeared the first number of *The Irish Felon*, a title intimating that liberty could only be conquered against law, in which James Fintan Lalor went for the absolute independence of Ireland.

"The principle," he said, "I state, and mean to stand upon, is this: that the entire ownership of Ireland, moral and material, up to the sun and down to the centre, is vested of right in the people of Ireland; that they, and none but they, are the landowners and lawmakers of this island, and that this right of ownership may and ought to be asserted and enforced by any and all means which God has put in the power of man. The entire soil of a country belongs of right to the entire people. The land question contains, and the legislative question does not contain, the materials from which victory is to be manufactured. Victory follows that banner, and no other. This island is our own, and have it we will. There can be no right of property in eight thousand, against the property, security, independence, and existence of eight millions, to take their food and give them famine, to take their home and give them the workhouse. Such rights are the code of the brigand, and can be enforced only by the hangman. War to their destruction or my own."

In the second number of *The Irish Felon*, Lalor declared for two objects—the abolition of the British Government, and the formation of a national one.

"Link repeal to the land, like a railway-carriage to its engine; ages have prepared it. Thus repeal will carry itself, like a cannon-ball down hill."

In the third number, July 8, 1848, Lalor rehearsed the "Faith of a Felon":

"Refuse all rent, except what remains after subsistence. Defy ejectment. The English Government must then either surrender the landlords, or support them with the armed power of the empire. If it surrenders the landlords, then the people are lords ; if it supports them, and attempts to carry the whole harvest of Ireland, we must oppose passive resistance, break up roads, break down bridges, and on occasion try the steel. Such a war would propagate itself throughout Europe.

"The right of the people to make laws was the first great moral earthquake.

"The right of the people to own land is the next.

"I will place Ireland in the van of the world, and set her aloft in the blaze of the sun."

The Irish People, on the same lines, was started in Dublin by James Stephen, in 1863, and suppressed in 1865. It urged the masses to give even their clergy the go-by, and trust to themselves. "There were three questions in Ireland—the Church question, the education question, the land question. The Church was an English question, education a Roman question, the land the Irish question."

In 1865, the American War ended, and a large number of disbanded Irish soldiers came to Ireland, and joined Stephen's movement.

In 1864, negotiations had been entered into to effect an alliance between Irish and English Liberalism, and the National Association of Ireland was founded for the Disestablishment of the Irish Church and alteration of the Land Laws; and in 1866 Mr. Bright was entertained at a public banquet in Ireland. Irish Nationalists and English Liberals were never on more cordial terms.

In 1868, Mr. Gladstone declared that "Ireland must be governed by Irish ideas."

In 1869, Mr. Gladstone's Disestablishment Bill was passed; and in 1870, the Peace Preservation Act and Land Bill.

In the autumn of 1871, Mr. Gladstone said at Aberdeen of Mr. Butt:

"When that learned gentleman makes his appearance in parliament, we shall all be very glad, and we shall be very anxious to discuss all about this matter of Home Rule. It will be an immense advantage in dealing with this question that its chief advocates should be there. It is in that way that in this country we deal with all political questions."

On September 1, 1871, "The Home Government Association," to include all parties, met in Dublin. On the 20th, Mr. Isaac Butt, leader of the Home Rule movement, was elected by Limerick, and in 1873 the programme of the party requiring an Irish parliament was published. The population was now (April) 5,400,000.

In 1871 and in March and July, 1874, and in 1875, motions for Home Rule were defeated in Parliament; on August 6, 1875, on the occasion of the centenary of O'Connell's birth, there was much dissension between the clerical and Home Rule parties, and in November the centenary committee was dissolved.

"The Gladstone Ballot Act" (1872), says Mr. T. P. O'Connor in "The Parnell Movement" (p. 225), "transcended in importance any other of the great acts of his first premiership; it gave the real voice of Ireland some opportunity of making itself heard."

At the 1874 election, the Home Rule advocates were seated in Parliament, under the generalship of Mr. Butt. It, however, became more and more apparent that if the Irish were to do any good in the House, they must form an Irish party outside and above all English parties.

In 1875, the man began to come to the front who has always known what was, from the Irish standpoint, the right thing to do, and how to do it. He it was who made English government incompatible in the same House with Irish misgovernment. He it was who would not permit English home rule without Irish. He roused, and helped others to rouse, the ten millions of Irish elsewhere, by his mission to America, his address to their House of Representatives, and the movement in Australia. After the three bad harvests, and the "exterminations," he taught even House of Commons Christians that Irishmen are of as much value as cattle and acres. He made Ireland a continuous Cabinet question, by making it a question of breaking Cabinets up; he wrought and welded the Irish phalanx into unity, till they rendered possible home rule for both nations, brought down to the meanest apprehension the difference between the "provincial" conception of local self-government and the glorious one of national self-government, and at last, having dictated terms in the capitol, makes them terms of peace between the two nations.

The great characteristic, however, of the Parnell movement is, that whilst it makes the land the basis of the movement in Ireland, it makes a policy of parliamentary action and obstruction the basis in England.

Mr. T. P. O'Connor best states the all-important Irish point of view as to the policy of obstruction in the House, and the question of land and rent:

"One of the great forces which had inspired the hope and strength which made the new movement possible, was the spirit excited throughout Ireland by the attitude of Mr. Parnell and Mr. Biggar in the House. The scenes—vexatious, indecorous, wanton, or boorish, as they appeared to the English public—were to the people of Ireland the electric messages of new hopes. Every word of those scenes was read with fierce and breathless eagerness. The representatives of a country trodden under foot for centuries were seen in the citadel of the enemy, aggressive and defiant. The Parliament that trampled upon every Irish demand for so many generations was seen raging in hysteric and impotent fury against two determined men. The movement that starts from 1879 will not be understood unless the fact is grasped that Ireland at that moment was living under the burning glow of parliamentary obstruction. The temper which this fact produces was the original impulse in preventing the farmers of 1879 from lying down dumb, helpless, and cowering under eviction, famine, and plague, as had been done by their fathers in 1846-7.

"Mr. Parnell was rapidly becoming the idol of the people, who could fuse their passions and affections into a united and mighty effort.

"How was the emergency of deepening distress, of ever-advancing famine, and ever-increasing eviction to be met? And now I have come to one of the cross-roads of my story. All that I have written will have failed if the reader do not see the road to take at this crisis, clearly marked out as with an iron finger. 1846-7 are the background of 1879-80. 1846-7 left two memories—of terrible suffering, and how it was submitted to. There has been no feeling so bitter as that much of the awful suffering could have been prevented if the people only had had courage to act in self-defence; to refuse to allow food to be exported from a starving nation; to refuse impossible rents that one man might luxuriate in the hour of national cataclysm, and that tens of thousands might perish in the agonies of hunger and of typhus fever; to refuse submission to decrees of eviction, death, or exile from lands brought to fertility by their toil, from houses built in their own sweat and blood and tears. The principle involved is indeed one that has passed from the region of debate to that of the jurisprudence of more than one nation. Anybody who will take the trouble to read the debates on the Compensation for Disturbance Bill will find instances given from the laws of Rome, Scotland, and Canada, in which stress of season is held to modify all contracts for rent. In the case of Ireland the whole controversy resolves itself into the question — rent or nation?"[1]

Mr. Parnell (Charles Stewart) was born in 1846. Sir John Parnell, his great-grandfather, held for many years the office of Chancellor of the Exchequer in the Irish Parliament, and resigned rather than vote for the Union. Sir Henry (Sir John's son) served many years in the English Commons, and became Lord Congleton in 1841.

In 1875, Mr. Parnell was returned to Parliament, and

[1] "The Parnell Movement," pp. 303-5.

in 1876 engaged in one or two stubborn conflicts with the Government. In February, 1877, he introduced "The Irish Church Act Amendment Bill," to facilitate purchase of their holdings by the tenantry of the disestablished Church, and was beaten by 150 to 110.

In the Prison Bill, the Mutiny Bill (flogging clauses), and again in the South Africa Bill, he developed thoroughly the "active," or "obstructive," policy in the House.

At a conference of the Irish party, in January, 1877, when Mr. Butt's policy was compared with Mr. Parnell's, the latter said that:

"If we had to deal with men capable of listening to fair arguments, there would be every hope of success for the policy of Mr. Butt, as carried out in past sessions, but we are dealing with political parties who really consider the interests of their political organizations as paramount beyond any other consideration."[1]

At the annual convention of the Home Rule Confederation, at the close of this year, Mr. Butt was deposed and Mr. Parnell elected in his place.

It was the habit of many farmers of Mayo, Galway, and Donegal to go to England for the harvest, earning about £100,000, which went not to their wives and families, but to the landlord. The loss of these men in 1877 is calculated by Dr. Wilson Hancock at £250,000.

In 1878 Mr. Davitt promulgated his plan to drive owners of property out of the island by constitutional agitation on the principles of labour, but the most important part of Davitt's scheme was to get possession of local bodies throughout Ireland.

Butt's federal plans were now dismissed as absurd. Land, it was said, must be the basis, and let occupiers be allowed to purchase their lands or relegate landlords to another solution. They should begin with absentees ("the country swarmed with them"), especially with the Eng-

[1] "The Parnell Movement," p. 279.

lish lords, and the London Companies, and stop evictions.

Davitt also instituted his enormous Vigilance Committees, following up his important scheme of 1878, to get possession of local bodies throughout Ireland. Davitt and Co. were going a longer journey than most Irish politicians, and on November 9, 1879, Messrs. Davitt, Daly, and Killen were arrested for seditious language.

It is best to resort to the same Irish writer as before, for a vindication which seems to me ample, of Mr. Parnell's conduct and policy at this crisis:

"After two famines," writes Mr. T. P. O'Connor, "the country was approaching a third. The following figures show the depreciation in the potato crop.

	Value.[1]
1876	£12,464,382.
1877	5,271,822.
1878	7,579,512.

But value in 1879 was only £3,341,028. In 1878, said the Registrar-General, the estimated quantity of potatoes in Ireland was 50,530,080 cwts., the average for ten years being 60,752,918 cwts., whereas the estimated yield for 1879 was only 22,273,520 cwts.

Compare with this the official figures of eviction.

1876	1269
1877	1323
1878	1749
1879	2667

The landlords of 1879 justified their traditions, the deeper the distress the more the evictions, and, as a climax, Mr. James Lowther was then Irish Chief Secretary.

The question was, under all these misfortunes, what should be done?

"Did the fact," says Mr. T. P. O'Connor, "justify a movement

[1] Thom's Directory.

against rent and eviction? If the farmer gave all the rent to the landlords, they would allow themselves to perish; if not, they were subject to eviction—wholesale starvation and wholesale eviction."

The first land meeting Mr. Parnell attended was at Westport, June 8, 1879. The resolution he spoke to was that:

"Whereas many landlords by successfully asserting in the courts their power to increase rents, irrespective of the value of the holdings, have rendered worthless the Land Act of 1870 as a protection to tenants; not only political expediency, but justice and the vital interests of Ireland, demand such a readjustment of the land tenure—based on the principle that the occupier shall be the owner—as will prevent further confiscation."

"In Belgium, Prussia, France, and Russia, the land," said Mr. Parnell, "has been given to the people—to the occupiers in some cases by revolution; in Prussia the landlords have been purchased out. If such an agreement could be made without injury to the landlord it would benefit the country."[1]

This, he said, was the final settlement. The immediate point was to resist eviction. He declared that a fair rent had been transformed by the failure of the potato into an exorbitant rent. "Now what must we do, in order to induce the landlords to see the position? You must show the landlords that you intend to hold a firm grip on your homesteads and land."[2]

In December, 1879, Mr. Parnell sailed for America, to raise funds for relief, and for the new organization; lectured before several State legislatures, and the House of Representatives at Washington, Lafayette, Kossuth, and another having alone had that honour before him.

In his manifesto to the people of America, he said, that now for the first time in history the landlords and the tenants of Ireland stood face to face. The next two

[1] "The Parnell Movement," p. 307.
[2] *Freeman's Journal*, June 1, 1879.

months would tell whether the conduct of the landlords would deprive them of all claim to the sympathy of civilization. If attempts at evictions were made on a large scale, it would take a thousand men to enforce the landlords' claims. If the prosecution were successful, and the leaders incarcerated, the peasants might despair of constitutional remedies.

The following extracts from Mr. Parnell's speeches in America and Ireland [1] show the policy of his mission, the power of his appeal, and the sympathy with which America responded:

"Well, we sailed for New York, and it was only on my entry to New York that I first commenced to appreciate the undeveloped power that is available for your succour, not only in the matter of charity, but in other matters of a very different nature if you call upon them. I feel confident that if you ever call upon them in another field and in another way for help, and if you can show them that there is a fair chance of success (enthusiastic cheering), that you will have their assistance, their trained and organized assistance." [2]

"We stand to-day in the same position that our ancestors stood. We declare that it is the duty of every Irishman to free his country if he can. We refuse to inflict needless suffering on the masses of our people. We will work by constitutional means as long as it suits us (great cheering). We refuse to plunge this country into the horrors of civil wars when she has not a chance; but I ask any true Irishman, priest or layman, whether he would not consider it the first duty to do what he could to enable his country to take her place among the nations of the world—to give their lives to the country that gave them birth. I call for no vain, no useless sacrifice; our present path is written within the lines of the constitution. England has given us that constitution for her purposes; we will use it for our own (loud cheers)." [3]

"It has given me great pleasure, during my visit to the cities of

[1] See Mr. Arnold Foster's "Truth about the Irish Land League," 1882.
[2] At Galway, October 25, 1881.
[3] At Waterford, December 6, 1881. *Freeman's Journal* report.

this country, to see the armed regiments of Irishmen who have frequently turned out to escort us. I thought that each of them must wish, 'Oh, that I could carry these arms to Ireland!' Well, it may come to that some day or other."[1]

"The fiendish works of eviction is still pursued, but from the blood of the brave Connemara women who resisted the home destroyers shall spring up a power which will sweep away not only the land system, but the infamous Government that maintains it."[2]

"With your help in keeping our people alive this winter we shall kill the Irish landlord system, and when we have given Ireland to the people of Ireland, we shall have laid the foundation upon which to build up our Irish nation. The feudal tenure and the rule of the minority have been the corner-stone of English misrule. Pull out that corner-stone, break it up, destroy it, and you undermine English misgovernment."[3]

On the 24th of September, 1881, *The United Ireland* said, "The convention has thrust Mr. Gladstone's Act aside. The Land League resumes its sovereignty and its purpose. If the Land Courts do its bidding, well; if they refuse to do it, better still;" and, Mr. T. P. O'Connor added, "Landlordism is dead. Gladstone's policy was to fix a relation between the landlord and tenant; the policy of the League was to abolish the relation."

The Land League placard was headed:

TO THE PEOPLE OF IRELAND.
Pay no Rent.
AVOID THE LAND COURT.
HOLD THE HARVEST.

How can they distrain for rent or tithes of a million of tenants?

"Now what are you to do to a tenant who bids for a farm from which his neighbour has been evicted? (Various shouts, 'kill him,' 'shoot him.') I wish to find out a better way which would give the lost sinner an opportunity of repenting. Shun him—on the

[1] At Cleveland, Ohio, January 26, 1881.
[2] At Pittston, February 16th.   [3] At Cincinnati, February 26th.

roadside, in the streets, at the shop counter, in the fair and market, and even in the house of worship, by leaving him alone as if he were a leper of old."[1]

"The objects of the Land League are very simple. First, to prevent rack-renting; second, to enable tenants to become owners of their own farms by paying a fair rent for a limited nnmber of years; third, to facilitate the working of the Bright clauses of the Land Act."[2]

"The present Chief Secretary, who was then all smiles and promises, would not have proceeded very far before he would have found that he had undertaken an impossible task to govern Ireland, and that the only way to govern Ireland is to allow her to govern herself. The English Government know that if they fail in upholding landlordism here—and they will fail—their power to misrule Ireland will go too."[3]

"The National Land League has plenty of money at its disposal for the purpose of defending the tenantry of Ireland in the court of law. Your fellow-countrymen in America will send you as much money as you want. Everywhere throughout the States I found the greatest anxiety to keep you. The day is dawning when we shall have taken the first great step to strike down British misrule, and the noble dreams of Grattan and of every Irish patriot ought to be brought to a triumph."[4]

"Now we are a party occupying an independent position in the House of Commons, pledged to remain aloof from every English party who will not concede the right of home government. We can push the policy just as far as we like. It is as sharp and potent for a party against the present Whig ministry as it was for a party of seven against the last Tory government."[5]

"They cannot suspend the Habeas Corpus Act without an Act of Parliament. They cannot pass a Coercion Act without an Act

---

[1] Mr. Parnell at Ennis.
[2] Mr. Parnell, Hansard, January 7, 1881.
[3] Mr. Parnell at Galway, October 1, 1881.
[4] Mr. Parnell at Beaufort, May 16, 1881.
[5] Mr. Parnell at Cork, October 4, 1881. *Irish Times* report.

of Parliament, and as long as we are able to stand in Parliament I will undertake to say they will pass neither the one nor the other (loud and prolonged cheering)."

On March 8, 1880, a dissolution of Parliament was announced, and there followed manifestoes from the three leaders, Lord Beaconsfield, Lord Hartington, and Mr. Gladstone, which defined the issues, stamped the spirit in which they have been since fought out by the Whig and Tory parties, but left the future open to the democracy of the three nations.

On the 9th, the Prime Minister's letter to the Duke of Marlborough, then Lord-Lieutenant of Ireland, proceeded as follows:

"Nevertheless, a danger scarcely less disastrous than pestilence or famine now distracts Ireland. A portion of its population is now attempting to sever the constitutional tie which unites to Great Britain. It is to be hoped that all men of light and leading will resist . . . this policy of decomposition.

"The power of England and the peace of Europe will largely depend upon the verdict of the country."

On the 11th, Lord Hartington issued his address. "He knew of no policy of decomposition. He believed Irish Home Rule to be impracticable and mischievous, and should continue to oppose it."

Mr. Gladstone's appeal to the nation partly foreshadowed his policy. He said:

"That those who endangered the Union with Ireland were the party that maintained there an alien Church, an unjust Land Law, and franchises inferior to our own; and the true supporters of the Union were those who firmly upheld the supreme authority of Parliament, but exercised that authority to bind the three nations by the indissoluble tie of liberal and equal laws."

The election soon after swept the Conservatives from power by the greatest defeat that ever befell an English political party.

On May 20, 1880, the Queen's Speech announced "the Peace Preservation Act for Ireland expires on the 1st June. You will not be asked to renew it"; and that the borough franchise in Ireland would be extended.

On March 31, 1880, Mr. Gladstone at Midlothian thought the "condition of Ireland one of peculiar prosperity," and spoke of the absence of crime and outrage; and Mr. Forster said we could govern Ireland by the ordinary appliances of the law.

The news of the dissolution reached Mr. Parnell on March 8th, when speaking at Montreal. Hastening home, Mr. T. P. O'Connor says that from the moment he landed in Ireland he proceeded to fight the election with an energy that seemed diabolic. He rushed from one part of the country to another, made innumerable speeches, and interviewed most of the candidates, was elected for three constituencies, and chose Cork city.

"In England and Scotland," writes Mr. T. P. O'Connor, "the general election had returned Mr. Gladstone to power. The masses of the Irish received the news with intense joy. The anti-Irish manifesto of Lord Beaconsfield had suggested the defeat of the Tories as the first duty of Irishmen everywhere. The leaders of the Home Rule confederation in England and Scotland issued a manifesto calling on the Irish electors to go solid for the Liberals. 'I went without my dinner,' said a Poplar Irishman to me, 'to vote for Mr. Bryce, and now he votes for coercion.' Liberals overflowed with affection for Ireland; but Mr. Parnell was no party to this blind adhesion to Liberals."

In July, 1880, the "Compensation for Disturbance Bill," the object of which was to check evictions, restrain landlords, and benefit tenants, passed the Commons, 295–217; but, on August 3rd, was rejected by the Lords, 282–51. By this Bill "any tenant of *not more than £30 yearly rent*, unable to pay by reason of bad harvests, and who could give security to the satisfaction of a County Court judge for payment of rent, should not be evicted for eighteen months." Lord Salisbury characterized this as "the measure of a mind not strongly impressed with reverence for the rights of property, and who desired to make his own path smooth by feeding wild beasts whom he is not strong enough to tame."

The rejection of his Disturbance Bill, with every mark of contempt from the Lords, together with the extraordinary number of evictions in that year, seem to have united Mr. Gladstone's heart for Ireland. In his great speech on this occasion the Premier establishes the following propositions: (1) Evictions increased with bad harvests; were a sentence of starvation; and that the bad harvests of 1877, '78, and '79 put the nation back to its state before the Land Act. (2) England had "legislated against the Irish tenants," and for their landlords, in a way unknown in England or Scotland, and which was almost a fraud on the Irish." (3) Fifteen thousand persons would be ejected in 1880, and in "enforcing processes by armies of State agents we were dangerously near civil war." (4) That crime diminished after the Land Act of 1870, and that the value of landlords' property improved.

Why, indeed, "in the circumstances," should Her Majesty's Government be carried on to supply English landlords with Irish rack-rents and victims?

The Whigs, however, thought the measure an inroad on the rights of property; and the death of the Bill produced the resignation of Lord Lansdowne; and, moreover, had a great effect on public opinion as to the House of Peers.

In September, 1880, Mr. Parnell proposed that tenants should become owners, after paying thirty-five years' rent. Mr. Parnell then appears to have thought he could force the hand of Parliament, and redoubled the Land League organization and agitation.

At Clonmel, October 24, 1880, Mr. Leamy declared

that there were "three great obstacles to national independence — Catholic disabilities till 1829, Protestant ascendency till 1870, and now foreign land tenure."

Mr. Bright, at Birmingham, on November 17th, argued that "force was no remedy"; and Mr. Chamberlain, on the Lord Chancellor's remark at the Mansion House, that "liberty and law were the two pillars of the State," said that "there were some men who would destroy liberty in order to preserve law. There was widespread disaffection in Ireland; there never was so much widespread disaffection in any country; but there was some just ground of grievance behind it."

On October 24, 1880, Mr. Parnell "took his coat off" for legislative independence; and on December 6th boasted that "in five or six years we shall have broken the power of the English Government to govern Ireland."

From 1879 to 1881 there was an enormous propagandism of American ideas; and American-Irish brains and gold helped the Irish agitation. The famine of 1847-8 had caused a vast increase of American-Irish, of whom the second generation became Americans first and Catholics afterwards; in fact, the abortive insurrection of 1848 changed the base of Irish revolution from Ireland to America.

With Irish home government, Irish interests would be to be quiet and loyal as part of the Britannic Empire, but by perpetuating an unreal union we risk a real separation. So early as twenty-three years after the *Mayflower* landed in 1620 at Cape Cod, the Irish emigration became numerous; hatred for England of course emigrated too, and, according to evidence got by Edmund Burke in Committee of the House of Commons, Washington's chief supporters in 1775 were Irishmen, born or descended. The Anglo-Irish policy of Whigs, clericals, and landlords, lost England the American Empire, and they are now endeavouring to lose our own.

In January, 1881, there were 25,000 English soldiers in Ireland, besides the so-called "Royal Irish Constabulary," which is not a constabulary at all, but an army of eleven to thirteen thousand of the finest troops in the world.

The year 1881 was perhaps the turning-point of Irish destiny, for acts of coercion and conciliation, of arrest and release, seemed to contend with one another, and in that year Mr. Parnell roused the American-Irish world, returned home a leader, was arrested, and came forth from prison, not to dictate terms to Government, for he did more — he took up the treaty of peace between England and Ireland—that treaty signed, sealed, and delivered by Grattan and England in 1782, and presented it again to the English Premier and nation for ratification.

On January 6, 1881, Parliament assembled, and the Queen's Speech stated:

"The social condition of Ireland has assumed an alarming character. The administration of justice has been frustrated, and an extended system of terror established. Proposals will be immediately submitted for entrusting me with additional powers. The Irish Land Act of 1870 has been productive of great benefits. I recommend the further development of its principles, both as regards the relation of landlord and tenant, and with a view to giving to a large portion of the people, by purchase, a permanent proprietary interest in the soil. This will require the removal of all obstacles arising out of limitations on the ownership of property. A measure will be submitted for county government in Ireland."

A message of peace and also a measure of coercion were then brought forward, the latter allowing arrest and imprisonment on suspicion. To the former, which was the Land Act, over eight hundred amendments were offered by the Irish Party, and on the 3rd of February thirty-six Irish members were suspended.

The Coercion (protection to life and property) Bill, and

the Arms Bill, became law on the 3rd and 2nd of March (1881) respectively. Proclamations were posted in Dublin and elsewhere, advising the people to discontinue partial outbreaks until the hour of action came. In the Manchester Free Trade Hall, Mr. Dillon declared that unless England changed her policy, Irishmen would be dogs and slaves if they did not long for the day when they could join another nation and send their representatives to Washington. At Trafalgar Square were great meetings against the Coercion Bill, and on the 20th of February Mr. Parnell said at Clare that if Mr. Forster wished to imprison all who favoured the land movement, his prisons would have to accommodate an enormous number, whilst the public opinion of the Irish people was fast becoming that of the world.

On April 7, 1881, Mr. Gladstone introduced his new Irish Land Bill. The old Bill of 1870 had done good service, but wanted development. There were three divisions of the subject, he said—the transfer and devolution of the land, the relations of landlord and tenant, and a group of matters requiring funds of the imperial exchequer. Land courts were inevitable, and judicial rents must be fixed for fifteen years without power of resumption by landlord, except by compulsory sale of the tenant's right.

Mr. Parnell recognized the Bill as an advance, as recognizing the principle of joint proprietorship between landlord and tenant. The Conservatives accused Mr. Gladstone of playing into the hands of the Land League and Mr. Parnell; they would keep to contract, free or forced, and trust to rack-rents and the Royal Irish Constabulary. In the eviction war of 1881, 17,341 persons were evicted. Over 30,000 soldiers were quartered in Ireland.

In May no less than six flying columns of troops supported authority in the disaffected districts, and in June Mr. Chamberlain, at Birmingham, said that:

"The Land Bill has been accepted by the representatives of Ireland, but that Mr. Parnell never concealed the fact that their chief object was not the removal of grievances, but separation of Ireland from England, and he would never have joined the Land League if he had not thought it would help him in the Nationalist and separatist movement. . . . Our talk never slackens; neither does agitation in Ireland."

When the Land Bill reached the Lords, the Duke of Argyll made his famous " jelly-fish " speech :

" His noble friends on the Government benches reminded him of a row of jelly fish, creatures beautiful in appearance, but destitute of backbone, and who, when seeming to be swimming, were only floating with the current."

In June the population was found by the census to have diminished one-ninth in ten years. In August the Land Bill passed. On November 5th, 2448 persons were in prison, but by November 12th, above 40,000 applications had been made to the Land Courts.

On August 27th Parliament was prorogued, and the Queen said :

" I warmly appreciate the zeal . . . maturing a measure for improving the relations between owners and occupiers of land in Ireland. It has been my study to use the exceptional powers confided to me in Ireland, by two Acts of this session, with vigilance and firmness, but with discrimination."

On the 26th of September Mr. Parnell made a triumphant entry into Dublin, and at a great torchlight procession of 100,000 people an address was presented to him :

" Honoured and beloved leader, in the name of the united people of Ireland, &c. As the great God who shapes the destinies of man has endowed you with wisdom, courage, and other attributes of a leader, we ask you to lead us on to that glorious consummation of national independence."

On October 13, 1881, Mr. Parnell was thrown into gaol; and on January 6, 1882, wrote from Kilmainham prison to acknowledge the freedom of the city of Dublin just presented to him and to Mr. Dillon.

There is no doubt that the Irish leaders had attempted, as Mr. Gladstone said at Leeds, "to intercept the operation of the Land Bill," but as Mr. Chamberlain explained at Leeds on the 25th of October, " the original objects of the Land League were legal, even praiseworthy. To stifle the agitation at that time would have been to have prevented reform."

Mr. Cowen so thoroughly and ably represents the cultured democracy of England, by which I mean the opinions and the will of the real thinkers and workers of England, that there need be no apology for introducing here several short extracts touching his views on Irish nationality *v.* English and un-English policy.

In 1881 he wrote as follows against Mr. Forster's coercion measures :

" I mean to oppose the Coercion Bill on every occasion and at every point. When all opportunity of defeating the principle has gone, I will strive to delay the operation by every fair, honourable, and legitimate process. When that resource is exhausted, I will assist in mitigating the harshness and minimising despotic powers. The Ministry will embitter the relations between England and Ireland."

The Irish Land Bill he heartily supported, repeating that the only safe way was to turn occupiers into owners. Writing to Mr. Parnell, April 14, 1881, he said he had read Mr. Gladstone's speech with pleasure. "If what was done and said during the coercion debates could be forgotten, I would be more sanguine of success."

Even in 1882, when Mr. Forster confessed that that measure failed through the influence of secret societies, when Government had reversed their coercion policy, and relieved Mr. Davitt and Mr. Parnell, and assassination threw back the country on the Prevention of Crime in

Ireland Bill, Mr. Cowen "faced the music" and said (May 23rd, p. 70 of his "Speeches"), "our Government of all governments may rest assured that their attempts to repress the legitimate and necessary expression of popular opinion will end in equal disaster. They can win the Irish people's hearts by just laws."

Mr. Cowen remarked (at Newcastle, on January 3, 1881, p. 189 of his "Speeches") on Irish nationality and character, and on British misrule, as follows:

"The desire for nationality is at the root of Irish discontent. There are at least 150,000 tenants on holdings, the annual average produce of each of which is not more than £25; but one bad season brings trouble, a second want, and a third starvation and insurrection. The affection of the Irish people may be won. There is less crime, as crime is commonly counted, than amongst any other people in Christendom. There is no race whose daughters are so virtuous or whose sons more valiant. The annals of France, Spain, Austria, England, and America are crowded with the achievements of brilliant captains sprung from the Irish stock. No people are more prosperous away from their own country, and few have a higher sense of veneration. Yet this race we cannot manage. I urged an Irish friend to go home and help Lord Bessborough to collect information. 'I will go home,' he said, 'but not to help any English constituted commission.' The literature on the subject is illimitable. 'I will go home and help to organize the most determined agitation, and then your government will perhaps utilize their pigeon holes. We will not conspire nor forget, but agitate. Many of us will be arrested, some imprisoned, and all decried as cowards and ruffians. But out of our imprisonment reform will come. Your selfish and soulless politician and your venal and ignorant press may howl till the crack of doom. If such be the result, our sufferings will be our countrymen's salvation.'"

On February 17, 1882, the Queen's Speech stated: "The condition of Ireland shows signs of improvement. Intimidation shows a diminished force. Have not hesitated to employ largely the exceptional powers for protection of life and property by the Acts of last session."

The Government had regarded as necessary both the suspension of the Habeas Corpus Act, the extension of peasant proprietary, and the reclamation of waste land.

In the debate on the Address, Mr. P. J. Smith moved an amendment in favour of the legislative independence of Ireland. Mr. Gladstone took part in the debate. I refer to his speech later on. It was on this occasion Mr. Mitchell Henry said that "this was probably the first time a responsible Minister of the Crown—certainly the Prime Minister—had really shown a desire to grapple with the difficulties of the question of self-government for Ireland." *The Times* next morning rated Mr. Gladstone for broaching the question of Irish legislative independence. Mr. Healy was discharged at the Cork Assizes, and declared that the movement for the abolition of landlordism was but preliminary to the overthrow of British government in Ireland; and Mr. T. P. O'Connor averred at Liverpool that landlordism was at its last gasp. The Executive proclaimed a number of districts, and nearly 700 men in authority, magistrates up to lord-lieutenants of counties, signed a declaration that law could not cope with lawlessness.

In this year the appointment of a Select Committee to inquire into the working of the Land Act was carried in the House of Lords by the Conservative party. Lord Salisbury was on the committee, and the report proposes a scheme of land purchase larger than that Mr. Gladstone has since put forth, and on terms more risky to the British taxpayer.

Mr. W. H. Smith also gave notice of a motion for legislation "to provide facilities to enable tenants in Ireland to acquire the freehold of the land in their occupation on just and reasonable terms"—those of the Lords' report.

In April, 1882, Mr. Parnell wrote to Captain O'Shea, one of the Irish members, and indirectly to the Government, that if the question of arrears could be introduced by way of relieving the tenants of holdings, and lessening greatly the number of evictions, and providing the purchase clauses of the Land Bill could be discussed, steps might be taken to lessen the number of outrages. The Kilmainham treaty followed, Messrs. Parnell, Dillon, and Kelly, were released on May 3rd, and Mr. Forster, who refused to be a party to "blackmail to lawbreakers," resigned.

After the assassinations of the 6th of May, the Crimes Act was passed and assented to on July 12th.

On the 30th of June there had been a long discussion in the Commons on this Bill, when twenty-three Irish members were suspended; and in July Mr. Parnell and the Home Rulers withdrew. About the 30th of that month seventeen counties were proclaimed. "There is a moral," writes Mr. T. P. O'Connor (July 8, 1882, "Gladstone's House of Commons," p. 236), commenting on the abstinence of the Irish members, and the consequent defeat of Government on the Crimes Act—"there is a moral in the whole business for the Irish people. The strong position taken up by some dozen determined and able Irish members made one of the greatest administrations and most powerful ministers bite the dust. If twelve good men could do so much, what would be the position of Ireland in Parliament if the Irish members represented truly the sentiments of the Irish nation and race? Let Ireland give Parnell seventy or eighty men at the next general election, and Parnell will be lord and master and dictator of the British Parliament!"

In 1882 Mr. Parnell took an active part in passing the Arrears Act; and in 1883, the Tramways and Labourers Acts.

The Arrears Bill passed on the 11th of August.

In August and September there was considerable disaffection, insubordination, and disorder amongst the police in Dublin, Cork, and Limerick.

On the 17th of October, the new Irish National League for self-government and land law reform held a national conference in Dublin.

On the 24th-27th of April, 1883, an Irish convention was held at Philadelphia, when Mr. Parnell's policy was adopted, and that of the dynamiters defeated. In September the National League invaded Ulster.

A convention of Irish delegates meeting in Melbourne, of which *The Times* gives the following account, showed how the question spread:

"A convention of Irish delegates from each of the Australian colonies was held in Melbourne in November, 1883, and over two hundred delegates, catholic dignitaries, members of the Victorian Parliament, of the Queensland Legislative Assembly, of the Legislative Assembly of Tasmania, and about twenty justices of the peace attended, and resolutions were passed affirming Home Rule, amendment of the Land Act of 1881 to facilitate the growth of a peasant proprietorship, equalization of the franchise to that of England and Scotland, and elective county government."[1]

"At the end of December, 1883,[2] Mr. Parnell arranged to hold a series of conferences with his colleagues at the beginning of 1884, as to extension of organization in Great Britain and Ireland, the policy of the party, electoral contests, and equalization of the franchise."

The Times also reports the Parnell demonstration and banquet of the 11th of December, the subscription to the tribute being £36,000, besides the American fund and the contribution from Australia. The Parnell testimonial, however, amounted to £38,000.

[1] *Times* Index, 1883, J. 1, 10, e.
[2] See *Times*, December 10th.

In 1884, the Irish National League Convention was held at Dublin, Mr. T. P. O'Connor, chairman, who urged renewed agitation against the Government.

On the 28th of February Mr. Gladstone introduced the Franchise Bill, adding to England 1,300,000 voters, to Scotland 200,000, and to Ireland 400,000, which, after great excitement, became law, together with the Redistribution Bill. On the 25th of June, 1885, a royal message proclaimed the triumph.

On the 1st of August, 1885, Mr. Forster stated at Bradford his belief that had the Compensation for Disturbance Bill passed the Lords, the whole question of the land would have been easier dealt with, the fierceness of the agitation would have been removed, and a final measure might have been passed without much difficulty.

The day however for expedients was done, as Mr. Gladstone convincingly set forth in May, 1886, by the following historical retrospect:

"We have tried expedients, our first repression or coercion; it is a medicine which we have been continually applying in increasing doses and with diminishing results. We have tried remedies. I refer now to the removal of religious disabilities, to the disestablishment of the Church, to the reform of the land laws, and to the removal or mitigation of the intolerable grievances under which Ireland used to labour with respect to education. We have not failed, for we have not finished. There is now a notion that something might be done by judicious mixtures of coercion and concessions; the very thing that we have tried. Go back to Catholic Emancipation. The Duke of Wellington proposed to open the door of Parliament to the Roman Catholics of Ireland, but at the same time disfranchised the 40s. freeholders. Sir Robert Peel in 1843-4 put O'Connell on his trial, but enlarged the endowment of Maynooth by an important Act for facilitating the grants of charitable bequests to the Roman Catholic Church, and by a third Act for the foundation of undenominational colleges. The whole course of the Government that came in in

1880, and was put out in 1885, was one rigid and incessant effort of judicious mixtures."[1]

The following documents and extracts, Mr. Gladstone's Home Rule for Ireland Bill, together with the certain response of the country, sufficiently show the drift of the situation. The making of the Irish nation and the consolidation of the Britannic Empire are one cause, and the greatest step towards both has now been irrevocably taken.

"I pledge myself, that in the event of my election to Parliament, I will sit, act, and vote with the Irish Parliamentary party; and if at a meeting of the party convened upon due notice specially to consider the question, it be determined by a resolution supported by a majority of the entire Parliamentary party, that I have not fulfilled the above pledge, I hereby undertake forthwith to resign my seat."[2]

"*New York*, August 16, 1885. The Committee of the Irish National League state that Mr. Parnell's party will be increased to eighty, and that it will then be enabled to establish a free Parliament in Ireland."[3]

"*Boston*. The leading Irish democratic organ, *The Pilot*, publishes plans for raising £45,000 at January Convention next, to enable Mr. Parnell to pay ninety Irish members £100 each annually for five years."[4]

"But I go back to the consideration of the great question of national self-government for Ireland. We cannot ask for less than the restitution of Grattan's Parliament with its important privileges and wide and far-reaching constitution."[5]

"Conscientiously opposed to a separate Parliament for Ireland, believing as I did and do that it would be absolutely ruinous to

---

[1] *Times* report.
[2] Parliamentary pledge of Parnellite members, *Times* Index, 1885, 26 d., 5 d.
[3] *Times* Index, 1885, 17 a., 4 c.
[4] Ibid. 25 s., 5 f.
[5] Parnell's speech at Cork, January 21, 1885, *Times* Index, 1885, 22 j., 10, 8.

the best interests of Ireland as well as dangerous to the security of England, I cannot alter my conviction on the main point."[1]

"In demanding the Disturbance Bill," says Mr. T. P. O'Connor, in "The Parnell Movement," "Mr. Gladstone alleged the horrible events attending the eviction of 15,000 people, but in 1881 17,341 persons were so deprived, and the greater proportion thrown on the roadside. Horse, foot, and artillery took part in the work of eviction, and sometimes the blue-jacket and the war vessel. A fit of frenzy passed over Ireland during the winter of 1881 and the spring of 1882. The country—with speech and writing and organization suppressed—stood at bay, and a wild and horrible wave of crime passed over it. The whole legislation of the Ministry had broken down; the Coercion Act had not put down crime; the Land Act had not closed the Land Question. The leaders of the Land League had declared all along that peasant proprietary was the only final and practical settlement of the Land Question.

"Conservatives then began to propose hostile motions against both measures, and endeavoured to 'filch and adopt' the Irish leaders' land scheme. The failure of coercion was acknowledged. Mr. Forster and Lord Cowper resigned, and 'Mr. Gladstone received the proposals of Mr. Redmond's new Land Bill with favour'" (p. 486).

Mr. Trevelyan's description of Orange demonstration is that :

"At their last meeting at Dromore sackfuls of revolvers were left behind, the reason . . . that an officer was seen to search the Orangemen. The Orange meetings, therefore, were bodies of armed men, many prepared to use their arms; some prepared to make a murderous attack upon the Nationalists. So far as the Government knew, it was not the custom of the Nationalists to go armed to their meetings until the bad example of the Orangemen."[2]

The inference surely seems, as Mr. T. P. O'Connor puts

[1] Letter from the Right Hon. Joseph Chamberlain, *Times* Index, 29 s., 6 b.
[2] Hansard, vol. cclxxxiv. p. 383.

it, that the Government that allowed such things was rather a stimulus to civil war than an obstacle.

Mr. O'Connor develops at some length his showing how the Lord-Lieutenant, Deputy-Lieutenant, and magistracy of Ulster were allowed to proclaim incitements and to make preparations that would lead to murder; and how at last, when Lord Spencer woke up, he sent police shorthand writers to some of the Orange meetings as previously to all the Nationalist meetings, and how the peers and magistrates at once abandoned their tone. He even ordered a body of police to prevent a breaking up of a meeting by Orange rowdies.

Thus the last effort at English ascendency in Ireland passed away, and the measure for enfranchising Ireland, described a year before by Lord Hartington as little short of madness, was passed, through Mr. Brodrick's folly in pressing an amendment, by 332 to 137, " probably the largest majority ever recorded in favour of an extension of popular liberties." Mr. Forster then suggested to reduce the number of Irish representatives from 103 to 81.[1]

From the day of Mr. Forster's Coercion Bill, the Irish members, says Mr. T. P. O'Connor, had set before their minds the destruction of the Liberal Ministry as their first political duty. In 1880, Liberals stood at 351; Conservatives, 238; Home Rulers, 63; but the Home Rulers did not remain a united party. In 1882 the Clôture Division left ministers a majority of 39. On May 13, 1884 (Vote of Confidence), it sunk to 28, and on February 27, 1885, to 14. On May 13, 1885, Mr. Gladstone announced the proposed re-enactment of certain provisions of the Crimes Act of 1882, and on June 8th (on the Budget) his Government ceased to exist.

Mr. John Morley then wrote [1] of " the peremptory dissipation of favourite illusions as to the Irish vote not counting."

[1] *Macmillan's Magazine*, p. 233, July, 1885.

"The notion that the two English parties could establish an agreement, that if either of them should be beaten by Irish auxiliaries, the victors should act as if they had lost, had been cherished by some not exactly simpletons. This fancy must be banished to the same limbo as the similar dream that Ireland could be disfranchised, and reduced to the rank of a crown colony. As for the new government, Parnell's vote has installed them, it can displace them; it has its price, and the price will be paid. The Irish not only count; they almost count for everything."

"Mr. Parnell and his party had," says Mr. T. P. O'Connor, "always declared that the destruction of the Liberal Ministry would mean the mitigation or abandonment of coercion, but when overthrown, a number of Liberal ministers were transformed from coercionists to enemies of coercion. On June 8th the Government had been overthrown. On June 17th Mr. Chamberlain, at Holloway, denounced the whole system of government in Ireland; although Mr. Gladstone, writing to Sir M. Hicks Beach, announced that the Ministry had practically agreed on coercing Ireland before their expulsion!"

"1885 came to be one of those years which bring the Irish face to face with ruin. Once more the great primordial battle of Irish life had to be fought out—the battle of rent, and under the Crimes Act every blow against the exaction of the uttermost farthing of rent would have been checked by coercion magistrates."

On November 14, 1885, the Parliament of 1880 was dissolved, and Mr. Parnell declared henceforward for one plank only—legislative independence. Mr. Chamberlain declared for the acquisition and distribution of land by local bodies, for free schools, and disestablishment. For two years previously the most energetic efforts had been devoted to the organization of the Irish vote in England, and it was a powerful factor in lessening the Liberal majority. Lord Richard Grosvenor said:

"The main cause is the Irish vote. They (the Tories) know that but for the imperative orders of Mr. Parnell and his friends, the Liberal majority would have been near 100."

To this add Mr. Parnell's portentous disclosure, made on the 8th of June, of the last elections' secret history:

"We had every reason to know that the Conservative party would have offered Ireland a statutory legislature, with a right to protect her own industries, and that this would have been coupled with the settlement of the Irish Land Question, on a lease of purchase, on a larger scale than that now proposed by the Prime Minister."[1]

Mr. Gladstone is the only statesman since Fox who has had the will, the capacity, and the occasion to grapple with the Irish danger, and to construct where others have destroyed; and the storm of misrepresentation and untruth which met the mere hint three or four years ago should have taught us what to expect now. It was during the session of 1882 that Mr. Gladstone uttered these much canvassed and ominous words:

"I wish to point out to hon. gentlemen that neither they, nor, so far as I know, Mr. Butt before them, nor O'Connell before him, ever distinctly explained the manner in which the real knot of this question was to be untied. 'The principle on which they profess to proceed is that purely Irish matters are to be dealt with by a purely Irish authority, imperial matters to be left to the imperial authority of a Chamber in which Ireland is to be represented. But they have not told us by what authority it is to be determined, which matters are Irish and which are imperial. Until they lay before the House a plan, in which they go to the very bottom of the question, and give us to understand in what way that decision is to be accomplished—the practical course of this subject cannot really be arrived at, and I know not how any effective judgment upon it can be pronounced."

Thrice before, in the House of Commons, Mr. Gladstone had referred to the same subject, besides doing so in his Guildhall, Midlothian, and Aberdeen speeches, and Lord Hartington during the present year, at the Eighty

[1] *Times* report, 8th of June.

Club, acknowledged that especially after the " increased definiteness" of his later speeches, no one could be surprised at his present tone.

But Mr. Gladstone gave still further emphasis in his manifesto when he declared that:

"I believe history and posterity will consign to disgrace the name and memory of every man, be he who he may, and on whichever side of the channel he may dwell, that having the power to aid in an equitable settlement between Ireland and Great Britain, shall use that power not to aid but to prevent or to retard it."

And at Edinburgh he made the famous declaration that:

"When once the wishes of Ireland shall be constitutionally ascertained, it would be not only allowable but beneficial to the three countries, and to the empire at large, that everything should be given to Ireland in the way of local self-government which is consistent with the maintenance of the unity of the empire, and the authority of Parliament connected with the unity of the empire."

With regard to the cost, difficulties, and indignity of carrying on Irish local investigation and local government in Westminster, they are at once endless and inappreciable except to those concerned in them. They are ably set forth in the Rev. Malcolm MacColl's pamphlet.[1] The Lords had already committed themselves, in 1882, with the concurrence of the whole Liberal party to a considerable Land Purchase Scheme, and in 1885 Lord Salisbury's Government passed a Land Purchase Act empowering the Treasury to borrow £5,000,000, and advance it to the Land Commission for the purchase of Irish estates, that sum being only an instalment.

All parties are, therefore, committed to the principle of a Land Purchase Scheme, and when two-thirds of Irish rental is spent elsewhere, what so great hardship can

---

[1] Pp. 32, 33.

there be in compelling the landlords concerned to change their investments?

The Domesday Book of 1876 shows that 292 persons hold 6,459,000 Irish acres, and the report of 1872 shows that of landlords owning over 100 acres each, nearly half or 4,842 were non-resident, and 5,589 resident.

The principle of the Tory measure of 1885 was that the process of sale should go on as long as there were landlords willing to sell, and tenants to buy. The Gladstone scheme of this year specially excludes mansions, demesnes, woodlands, grazing lands, &c., meeting the only valid objections to forced sales. When there is, on the one hand, a nation in ruin and insurrection for want of land, and when, on the other, the buying out of 292 persons would return 6,459,000, or one-third of the national acreage, to the nation; and when, moreover, out of 10,431 owners of over 100 acres each, 4,842 are already non-resident, it is obvious that more than half the national acreage is merely a question of investment, and that 292 persons cannot stand in the way of the nation. Such a scheme can hurt no man living, and offend no man's liking or love for the soil.

During the Gladstone epoch, the question has already passed through various stages, all of increasing intensity. By postponing the settlement of the land, we bound the question of nationality and land together irrevocably, and envenomed both. We have quietly seen accumulate in Ireland, and we have helped to accumulate, all the elements of unity, and yet have ignored or obstructed their necessary consummation.

We have had to abandon the landlords because we would not abandon their monopoly, and we have had fixity of tenure conquered, as O'Connell warned us nearly forty years ago it would be conquered, "by an accumulation of murders."

It was the American Irish, that is, the "Irish emigration," sent there by our tyranny, that beat us out of

America. The remittances to Ireland from Irish settlers in the United States and British North America have amounted between 1848 and 1884 to £29,776,977; and the 1880 census shows 1,854,571 natives of Ireland then living in the United States.

The English people have risen to the full height of the reason of State, plain enough ninety years ago to the intellects of Grattan, Burke, Fox, and Sheridan, that what we have to do is to make sound and heart-whole the Irish nation, as a nation, because without that, our triune home empire, the basis of our vast imperial superstructure, is not broad enough to carry it. England's mighty trilateral—England, Scotland, Ireland—is as yet fatally incomplete, and in a great war would infallibly let in the foe. Let us understand that implacable question, or rather that supreme fact and factor, of Irish nationality, and not dream that because we have freed the Catholics, Ireland is less united, or less a nation, or that because we have partly freed the land, Irish nationality is less strong, or that Ireland is less free to demand her freedom. The more united and free Ireland becomes, the stronger becomes her nationality. What then shall we do with it? Her nationality is herself. You must exterminate it or exalt it. For what are we prepared, if not to give her some constitutional guarantee that her existence as a free and equal sister nation is recognized?

Nationality and the land, then, have been and remain the supreme motives of Ireland, and we have met them with a policy of bankruptcy for the one, and a policy of despair for the other. In all nations there is a direct indefeasible relationship between the land and the people. Unless the latter possess the former, *it cannot be constituted*, for together alone they form one normal whole.

On Mr. Parnell, Home Rule, and the situation, hear Mr. Joseph Cowen, M.P., as he spoke at Newcastle-on-Tyne, December 22, 1883:

"Can agitators light fire without fuel, or sustain a revolution without reason? It never was done. It never will be done. . . . To convict the people is to condemn the Government. . . .

"If we tried crown colony rule, remonstrances would come thick and fast from America and the Colonies. If these were discarded, something more serious might follow. There is an invisible power in Irish politics which no Coercion Acts can reach. . . . The steady active hatred of eight or ten millions of Irishmen wielding great political power in America might involve us in a time of trouble. Home Rule means improved union, not separation. When there are eighteen independent parliaments in the British dominions, it is only prejudice to contend that another would make the difference between union and dismemberment. We have tried to rule Ireland by army, Church, and landlords, and failed. Let us now try to rule her by her own people."

It is also worth while to read Mr. Blake's speech on Canadian Home Rule and Imperial Federation, April 20, 1883. It was a speech made by him as leader of the Liberal party in Canada, and on the Irish question shows, as Mr. McCarthy says, how

"The magical influence of self-government has converted Canada from the distracted home of conflicting and disaffected populations, torn by religious animosities and political hatreds, and only approaching a common feeling in their animosity to the English Government—has converted Canada from that miserable hopeless condition into one of the best ordered, most prosperous, most rising, and most united countries on the earth."

Yet the British North America Act for the Federation of the Dominion of Canada came into operation as late as 1867.

England and Ireland both want and must have something that shall first make sure the salvation of our home nationalities, and then make certain our premiership of the world. We want and will have that which shall glorify the spirit of the Irish nationality, and make the nucleus of our mighty empire eternally safe and free. England without Ireland, it has gone forth to the world; England without Ireland, or with Ireland justly estranged, is nothing, rather, as Montalembert said, " an eternal avenging death-sore." Such an Ireland, moored as she is alongside England, would be in the next great war but a landing-place for our foes, whence old England would be raked from stem to stern, with an invincible nationality, a fourth of our territory, and a seventh of our population against us!

On the whole of this land-logic and nation-logic, note the words of John Bright:

"It is in the eternal decrees of providence that so long as the population of a country are prevented from the possibility of possessing any portion of their native soil by legal enactments and legal chicanery, these outrages should be committed, were they but as beacons and warnings to call the legislature to a sense of the duties it owed to the country which it governed."

Or again, as he said at the Rotunda in Dublin, "A better parliament can alone improve Ireland. If there were 100 more members of parliament for large and free constituencies, your voice would be heard. 105 united members of parliament might do anything."

Let us, then, give to Ireland what every state in America has, what every province in Canada has, and what our Colonies practically have.

The Irish are what the English made them. Irish misery is Whig and Tory statesmanship; Irish happiness will now be the people's statesmanship. Omission and commission have done their worst. Not only, for instance, were we sinking and wasting half a million in a Thames tunnel whilst a quarter million would have formed a harbour in Galway, with depth and security to make it the Liverpool of Ireland; *but we should at one time have attempted even to destroy any existing Liverpool in Ireland*, as we did destroy every form of Irish industry that could compete with its fellow in England.[1]

What, then, do these seven hundred years of incapacity and outrage prove? What do those eighteen years, 1782–1801 prove? What do all things prove, but that Ireland can, and that England cannot, rule Ireland!

It is no business of mine to analyze the motives or asperse the conscience of those with whom it is to be hoped will be the Liberal future; but Mr. Chamberlain of all men ought to have known that the essence of the Irish question is her nationality. Without that, mere local self-government can have neither mission, nor mandate, nor vital force. Mr. Chamberlain has emphatically repudiated Home Rule counsels in the shape of "a separate parliament for Ireland. I cannot alter my convictions on the main point."

All federal schemes between nation and empire can only be practically worked out by representation in an imperial parliament, and here Mr. Chamberlain is undoubtedly right.

In not subordinating Ulster to Ireland, however, he was, or is not, federal. For when nations and empire are to be federated, the more national the nations the more imperial will be the empire. Before unity you must have the units, and the sounder and completer the units the stronger the unity. Mr. Chamberlain cannot grasp this, or fails to act on it.

Mr. Chamberlain's fault throughout—the beginning and the end of his misconception—is here.

A nation is socially, politically, historically one. It is a sacred and indestructible essence. It has its sufficing unities of boundary, race, institutions, language, and ideas.

Ulster, Scotch and Protestant, was, as all the world

---

[1] See Lecky's "England in the Eighteenth Century," as to destruction of Irish woollen trade by English statute under William III.: "For nearly fifty years after, every bad season produced a famine."

knows, mechanically and forcibly introduced—thrust into the flank of Ireland, the natives being sent off "to hell or Connaught," and forbidden on pain of death to return. No nation can be disintegrated, no nation created, by a surgical process like that, unless it absorbs and destroys the other nation.

As the basis of radicalism is the freedom, initiative, and force of the individual; so the basis of federalism and empire is the freedom, wholeness, and force of the constituent nations.

"Seven-twelfths of the Protestants of Ireland live outside these three counties in the north-east corner of Ulster, and the other five-twelfths live inside those counties," said Mr. Parnell lately.[1] If so, would Mr. Chamberlain, or even Mr. Goschen, make of the five-twelfths, in a little corner, a nation?

No statesman destroys or questions real life. He knows that all true life helps all other true life. As well say that the free individual is necessarily hostile to family life, or that to a free commune, or a free commune to a self-governed country, or free countries and municipalities to national well-being, or confederation to empire—as well say all this as assert that the Irish nation, in life, dignity, honour, and independence, can "be dangerous to the security of England." That were Whig or Tory statesmanship; but Liberal, Radical, Irish, or English statesmanship—never! Life is only dangerous to those who would, but cannot, destroy it.

In the debate of the 1st of June last, Mr. Chamberlain produced his Canadian plan as the one to be applied to Ireland, and as having the effect of protecting Ulster, but the Chancellor of the Exchequer showed that it would have the contrary result:

"In the 91st section of the Canadian Act . . . the provincial

[1] *Times* report, June 8th.

legislature shall have exclusive authority over direct taxation with the province, the establishments, and tenure of provincial offices, and over the property (men of Ulster tremble) and civil rights of the province (cheers and laughter). . . . It may interest him to learn that the provincial parliament, which is to be the model for the Irish parliament, has exclusive authority over the administration of justice, the maintenance and organization of provincial courts, both civil and criminal (cheers and laughter). This is his last patent plan."[1]

Why, according to Alison's partial life of Castlereagh, "the most formidable opposition (to the Union) was among the barristers and citizens of Dublin, the country gentlemen all over Ireland, and the lower ranks of the Orangemen and Protestants of the North; with most of them it was not mere resistance, but absolute horror."

It is unnecessary to argue the question of Ulster; it is sufficient to state it.

Ulster as a plantation of Scotch Presbyterians has always been favoured as a garrison province, and has constantly presumed accordingly.

Ulster was foremost in all Ireland in sympathy with the American rebellion; was aroused as one man against English dictation during the volunteer movement; was drawn over by Castlereagh and Pitt by notorious means; and has always known better than the rest of Ireland how to protect herself against landlord tyranny and greed.

"Protestant" Ulster has always endeavoured and endeavours still to monopolize, against "Catholic" Ulster, all municipal offices and representation.

"Protestant" Ulster is exclusive, domineering, and would be dominant. "Catholic" Ulster is liberal, conciliatory, and, as to all questions but nationality, yielding.

Mr. W. A. O'Conor has some very pertinent observations on "Orangeism" (pp. 69, 70), in his recent volume "The History of the Irish People":[2]

[1] *Times* report, June 2, 1886.   [2] Heywood, 1886.

"The first Orange lodge was formed on the 21st of September 1795.

"The impunity accorded to Orangemen had a very real meaning. The dominion of England could not (formerly) be maintained for a day in Ireland without their aid.

"There was at once safety and danger in Orangeism. The part which the Protestants had taken in 1798 was to be prevented in the future at any cost. Orangeism might be relied on to destroy Catholics, but its tendency was towards insubordination, its loyalty being conditional. The vain effort was therefore made to appease it by satiating its hatred. O'Connell always said that rather than remain in the union, he would be satisfied to repeal Catholic emancipation, and trust himself to his Protestant fellow countrymen. Against these dispositions Orangeism must be fostered. As it had been created by government, all that was needed was to give it legal strength, and let it follow its own will. It was supplied with congenial magistrates and arms."

Upon this point of Catholic *v.* Protestant there is some valuable information in a speech by Mr. Charles Dawson, ex-Lord Mayor of Dublin, and ex-M.P. for Carlow, at the Rotunda on May 12, 1886. He showed that in the treatment of minorities the Irish have been almost without reproach. That immediately following Catholic emancipation the Catholic constituencies used their newly-acquired power to return forty-three members of Parliament who were Protestants. That being a minority in religion has been a password instead of an obstruction to the favour and confidence of the Catholics. In the matter of municipal honours, the generosity of the Catholics has been unbounded. In the Catholic city of Cork the first Reform election secured nine Protestant Councillors, and the second Mayor was a Protestant; since then there have been several Protestant Mayors in succession. Last year there were eight Protestant members of the Harbour Board. Mr. Dawson says:

"There are more Catholics in proportion in Belfast than there are Protestants in Dublin. Have they had, or have they now, a Catholic member of their Council? Have they now, or have they ever had, a Catholic Mayor, or a Catholic Sheriff, or a Catholic Treasurer, Engineer, or Officer of Health? Have they now, or have they ever had, any Catholic officer whatever, paid or honorary, first-class or lower? Protestant Ulster—which turns out on investigation to be a myth, inasmuch as the non-Catholics dominate only in certain districts—compares sadly in point of tolerance with Catholic Cork or Dublin, Limerick or Waterford. In Derry the power is entirely in the hands of the Protestants, although there is a majority of Catholics in the population. To 17,000 Catholics there are only 12,000 Protestants, and the Corporation of Derry has only one Catholic member. The Corporation does not employ one solitary Catholic in any department. In the whole of Armagh and Down no place of honour or emolument is given to a Catholic, and this is true of railways, banks, factories, poor law boards, &c. Coming to the Catholic districts of Donegal, Fermanagh, Tyrone, and Monaghan, there is not now, nor to my knowledge has there ever been, one single Catholic appointed to an elective position by the non-Catholic minority, who still have power over the Catholic people."

This certainly looks, as the Rev. Malcolm MacColl remarks in his able pamphlet, " as though the Orangemen of Ulster object to Home Rule, not because they fear persecution, but because they expect equality."

"Local Government in Irish counties is a gross and palpable mockery. The grand jury, who are mostly landlords or land agents, and generally Protestants, have the entire control of County Government. The pettiest Act for local purposes must be obtained from the Imperial Parliament at a great cost of money, time, and trouble. London robs the provinces, as old Rome robbed hers, of wealth, intelligence, and enterprise."

Moreover, all Irish matters that are not locally monopolized are either managed or jobbed from the Castle; for instance, elementary and intermediate education, the

Irish constabulary, the prisons, the Fishery Board, the Board of Works, including public buildings, harbours, inland waterways, advance of public money for land improvements, for drainage, for sanitary works, artizan's dwellings, &c. In our Lords' House, moreover, Ireland has only 28 out of 526 ; and in the Commons she is outnumbered 6 to 1, and always by men ignorant of Irish needs.

One word more about the man who almost alone, among English statesmen, seeks to do justice to Ireland. It is not the first time he has been assailed for so doing, and Earl Russell's reference to him in 1869 fits the present situation :

" I still retain my opinion that Mr. Gladstone, encountering great risks, and provoking bitter animosity, has aimed, not at official station, but at the welfare of his country in the mighty struggle in which he has engaged. If he should aspire to perform a permanent and immortal service to his country, to reconcile England and Ireland; if he should seek to remove the last link of the fetters fastened by the conqueror on the limbs of his victim, . . . then indeed he will be enrolled among the noblest of England's statesmen, and will have laid the foundations of a great work. I feel sure that Mr. Gladstone will not propose to take a leap in the dark. The wreath *ob civem servatum* will be a million times deserved by the minister who shall knit together three nations." [1]

Sir C. Gavan Duffy characterizes Mr. Gladstone's Irish endeavours as " one of the most courageous and disinterested achievements in human history. A statesman, when frame and brain need repose, takes in hand a task fit for Hercules. Before laying down his load of human responsibility, he braces his strength for one more supreme task for the service of the nations. A hundred years hence, this will perhaps be the most memorable fact in

[1] Earl Russell's 3rd letter to Mr. Fortescue, 1869.

English annals during the latter half of the nineteenth century."

The words, however, which Grattan applied to Fox were, and will remain, the supreme eulogy for such statesmanship as his and Gladstone's:

"What an idea has he disclosed as just and applicable to Ireland! An Irish legislature, and an Irish government; a genuine executive, and a genuine parliament, *major rerum nascitur ordo*. As an Englishman he would strengthen the connection by removing the motives of separation. This is an idea worthy a comprehensive statesman. He applies to great passions, and great principles, for the government of a great country. He stood, the Marpesian rock that struck its base to the centre, and raised its forehead to the skies!"

Let us add, in the words of Grattan, when he retired from the Irish Parliament:

"May the House of Commons flourish, but let the people be the sole authors of its existence, as they should be the great object of its care. May the connection with Great Britain continue, but let its result be perfect in the fairest and fullest sense."

It only now remains to add his supplication: "However it may please the Almighty to dispose of Princes or of Parliaments, may the liberties of the people be immortal!"

Everywhere and always throughout this controversy let us remember that the party of progress believes in development, not repression; and in conservatism, by development. The development of the threefold manhood of this empire should be no more and no less real, radical, and profound, than should be the development of the three or four home nations. Surely the English manhood has become imperial manhood, because it has been more symmetrical and complete than that of other nations. In like manner the English nations and Colonies can better enter into empire, because they are more self-governed, national, and complete than colonies and nations elsewhere.

Thus alone can the mighty unknown future, to which confederation points, be built up. Thus alone can the mightiest of all mundane forces, "the coming democratic confederation of all the Britains," be rightly brought together and held together—be best united to each other and to the whole around the throne of England.

This book cannot close without an extract (which I am forced to condense) from the Premier's short history of ninety years of the Anglo-Irish question, and of its black traditions; without reference also to his golden vision of the future, and its glorious hopes!

"There was such a golden moment; it was in 1795, it was on the mission of Lord Fitzwilliam. At that moment it is historically clear that the parliament of Grattan was on the point of solving the Irish problem. The two great knots of that problem were emancipation and reform. The cup was at her lips when the hand of England dashed it to the ground, in obedience to the wild and dangerous intimations of an Irish faction. There has been no great day of hope for Ireland till now—more than ninety years. What Ireland was doing for herself in 1795, we at length have done. The Roman Catholics have been emancipated, slowly, sullenly, not from good-will, but from abject terror. The second problem has been also solved, and I am thankful to say with a free heart and open hand, and the gift of that franchise was the last act required to make the success of Ireland in her final effort absolutely sure. We have given Ireland a voice, we must all listen, divided, as I am afraid we are, by an almost immeasurable gap."

"You have power, wealth, rank—what have we? We think we have the people's heart! We believe, and we know we have the promise of the harvest of the future. The ebbing tide is with you, and the flowing tide with us. Ireland stands at your bar expectant, hopeful, almost suppliant. She asks a blessed oblivion, and in that our interest is deeper even than hers. My right honourable friend, Mr. Goschen, asks us to abide by the traditions of which we are the heirs. What traditions? By the Irish traditions? Go into the length and breadth of the world, ransack the literature of all countries—can you find a single book in which the conduct of England towards Ireland is treated except with profound and bitter condemnation. Those traditions are a broad black blot.

"Ireland also asks a boon for the future, which will be to us, in respect of honour, no less a boon than to her in respect of happiness, prosperity, and peace.

"Think, I beseech you, think well, think wisely; think, not for the moment, but for the years that are to come, before you reject this Bill."[1]

We may well pause before rejecting the words of the greatest man now living upon this planet, respecting the recognition of one of its most considerable facts—a fact, moreover, materially affecting the constitution of the most awful and glorious combination of political, social, and citizen progress and power that practical politicians can at present contemplate. We must prepare, through Gladstone, for another policy and a new epoch.

"To see, like some vast island from the ocean,
  The altar of the Federation rear its shape in the midst.
    .   .   .   Its shadows hid
  Far ships; to know its height the morning mists forbid.
  To hear the restless multitude for ever
  Around the base of that great altar flow."

[1] June 7, 1886.

This book is a preservation facsimile.
It is made in compliance with copyright law
and produced on acid-free archival
60# book weight paper
which meets the requirements of
ANSI/NISO Z39.48-1992 (permanence of paper)

Preservation facsimile printing and binding
by
Acme Bookbinding
Charlestown, Massachusetts

2008

www.ingramcontent.com/pod-product-compliance
Lightning Source LLC
Chambersburg PA
CBHW020827230426
43666CB00007B/1128